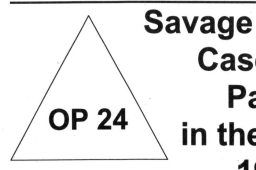

Savage
Case Studies of Pacification in the Philippines, 1900–1902

Robert D. Ramsey III

Combat Studies Institute Press
Fort Leavenworth, Kansas

Library of Congress Cataloging-in-Publication Data

Ramsey, Robert D., 1946-
   Savage wars of peace : case studies of pacification in the Philippines, 1900-
1902 / Robert D. Ramsey III.
      p. cm. -- (Long war series occasional paper ; 24)
   Includes bibliographical references.
   1. Philippines--History--Philippine American War, 1899-1902. I. Title. II.
Series.

   DS679.R36 2007
   959.9'031--dc22

                                                              2007028938

For sale by the Superintendent of Documents, U.S. Government Printing Office
Internet: bookstore.gpo.gov Phone: toll free (866) 512-1800; DC area (202) 512-1800
Fax: (202) 512-2104 Mail: Stop IDCC, Washington, DC 20402-0001

ISBN 978-0-16-078950-2

Foreword

Consider the following: The United States is engaged in what some political and media leaders call an immoral war, a war that did not have to be fought. After a relatively easy initial conquest, the US Army finds itself faced with armed resistance to US occupation. US strategic goals have changed since the war began; domestic political opposition increases as insurgent activities prolong the war. Insurgent leaders monitor US domestic politics and adjust their strategy accordingly. US Army Soldiers adapt to the uncertainty and employ novel techniques to complex military and nonmilitary problems in a land where they are strangers and about which they have little understanding. Does this sound familiar? It should, but this description does not depict events from 2003 to 2007 in the Middle East—it describes events from 1898 to 1902 in the Philippines.

Combat Studies Institute (CSI) is pleased to publish its 24th Long War Series Occasional Paper, *Savage Wars of Peace: Case Studies of Pacification in the Philippines, 1900–1902*, by CSI historian Robert Ramsey. In it he analyzes case studies from two key Philippine military districts and highlights several themes that are relevant to today's ongoing operations in the Long War. Between 1899 and 1902 the US Army was successful in defeating Filipino resistance to American occupation using what military leaders at the time called a combination of attraction and coercion. However, success came only after initial setbacks, disappointments, and significant changes in leadership, military strategy, and political adaptation.

In the two regions of the Luzon Island analyzed in this occasional paper, Army leaders employed a mix of political and economic incentives, combined with military actions and strict martial law to subdue the resistance. The geographic isolation of the *insurrectos* on the Philippine archipelago was also an advantage for US forces. The capture of key *insurrecto* leaders provided critical intelligence, and their post-capture pledge of support for the new government helped break the resistance by 1902.

This work highlights, among many other themes, the importance of perseverance, adaptability, and cultural understanding. Written at the request of the Command and General Staff College for use in their curriculum, we believe this occasional paper will be a valuable addition to the professional development of all Army leaders. *CSI—The Past Is Prologue!*

Timothy R. Reese
Colonel, Armor
Director, Combat Studies Institute

Acknowledgments

No one completes a project such as this by himself. Among those requiring special thanks are US Army Command and General Staff College faculty member Dennis K. Clark for suggesting this project; Combined Arms Research Library archivist Elizabeth Merrifield for gathering materials in a short time; Dr. William G. Robertson and COL Timothy R. Reese for supporting this effort and for reviewing the manuscript; Robin Kern for making the maps; and Betty Weigand for her attentive editing that produced a better product. Without the support and effort of those above, as well as others, I could not have completed this work in the time permitted. However, as always, responsibility for errors in fact or judgment rests with me alone.

Contents

Maps

Tables

Chapter 1

The American Conquest of the Philippines, 1898–1900

> What nation was ever able to write an accurate programme
> on the war upon which it was entering, much less decree
> in advance the scope of its results? Congress can declare
> war, but a higher power decrees its bounds and fixes its
> relations and responsibilities. The President can direct the
> movement of soldiers on the field and fleets upon the sea,
> but he can not foresee the close of such movements or
> prescribe their limits. He can not anticipate or avoid the
> consequences, but he must meet them. No accurate map
> of nations engaged in war can be traced until the war is
> over, nor can the measure of responsibility be fixed till the
> last gun is fired and the verdict embodied in the stipula-
> tion of peace.

> President William McKinley, 16 February 1899[1]

President McKinley made the above remarks in his defense of
the United States (US) acquisition of the Philippines at the end of the
Spanish–American War. US Secretary of State John Hay described the
Spanish–American War as a brief, "splendid little war"[2] fought primarily over events in Cuba. However, American naval action at Manila Bay
required Army forces for service in the Philippines. A brief campaign by
the newly raised American VIII Corps, working with local Filipino forces,
defeated the Spanish in Manila by mid-August 1898. Uncertainty as to
American objectives created tension for months with the Filipino revolutionary government whose goal was independence. When the United States
purchased the Philippines from Spain in the Treaty of Paris of December
1898, the Filipino revolutionaries hoped the US Senate would fail to ratify
this unpopular treaty. Then, on 4 February 1899, war broke out between
the American units in Manila and the Filipino forces surrounding the town.
For the Filipino revolutionaries, the war would be two-phased: a brief conventional war of defeats followed by a protracted guerrilla war. For the
American Army in the Philippines, it would become a 40-month struggle
during which practically the entire US Army would see service.

This study will examine the attempts to pacify the Philippines by
focusing on the actions in two American districts on the island of Luzon. To
understand what American commanders confronted and their subsequent
actions, it is necessary to look at the setting of each area, the population,
the insurgent[3] organization, and the American Army operations. This first

1

chapter provides a brief background as context for the following two chapters. Chapter 2 focuses on the pacification of the Ilocano region in northwest Luzon, and chapter 3 focuses on the pacification of the Tagalog region in southwestern Luzon. In conclusion, chapter 4 provides an assessment of the two case studies. A chronology of events is provided in appendix A.

The Philippines

The Philippine archipelago—ceded by Spain after 330 years of occupation to the United States—lay off the coast of Southeast Asia. Its 3,141 islands were bounded by the Pacific Ocean to the east, Borneo and the Celebes Sea to the south, and the South China Sea to the west and north (see map 1).[4] The size of the area was slightly less than the eastern half of the United States. The land area was greater than the size of the New England states, New York, and New Jersey combined. The two islands of Mindanao and Luzon made up almost 75 percent of the land area.[5] Of volcanic origin and prone to earthquakes, the islands were mountainous with narrow coastal plains and interior valleys and plains. Although it varied by elevation, the vegetation was tropical with jungle, thick vegetation in low-lying swampy areas, and rice paddies in the plains. The archipelago had three seasons: dry and temperate from November to March, dry and hot from April to May, and rainy and humid from June to October. Typhoons were an annual occurrence. Diseases—malaria, dengue fever, dysentery, beriberi, smallpox, measles, leprosy—were common, particularly in the wet season, and periodic cholera epidemics occurred.[6]

Divided by ethnic, language, and religious differences, the Filipinos were not a homogenous people. The major ethnic groups were Negritos, Indonesians, Malayans, European mixed-blood mestizos, and Chinese. The Negritos, the initial inhabitants from New Guinea who lived in the mountains of most islands, had some 21 tribal names. The Indonesians, divided into 16 tribal groups, resided primarily on the island of Mindanao. The Malayans, by far the most numerous and most widespread throughout the archipelago, consisted of 47 tribes. Considered the "civilized races" by the Spanish, the Malayans were classified into several groups: Visayans—2.6 million, Tagalogs—1.7 million, Bicols—518,000, Ilocanos—442,000, Pangasinans—366,000, Pampangos—338,000, Moros—268,000, and Cagayanes—166,000. European mestizos, small in number but strong in influence, were primarily descendants of Spaniards. A small but economically influential Chinese community of 38,000 resided in the islands. Filipinos had no common language. Less than 10 percent of the population spoke Spanish. In 1898, 27 dialects were identified of which the

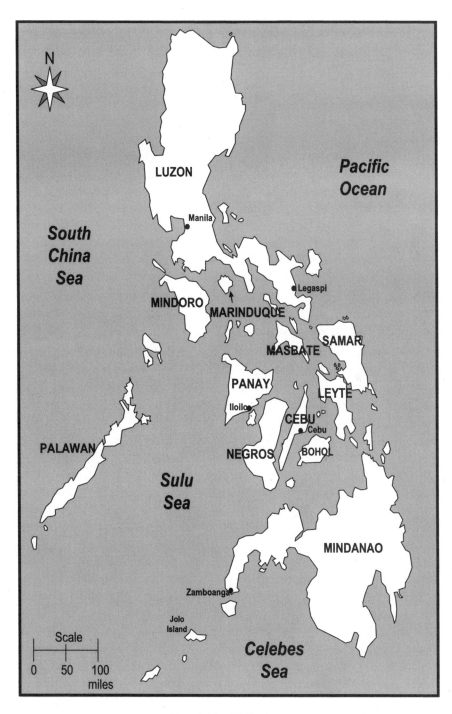

N

LUZON

Manila

Pacific
Ocean

South
China
Sea

MINDORO

MARINDUQUE

Legaspi

MASBATE

SAMAR

PANAY

Iloilo

LEYTE

CEBU
Cebu

PALAWAN

NEGROS

BOHOL

Sulu
Sea

MINDANAO

Zamboanga

Jolo
Island

Celebes
Sea

Scale

0   50   100
miles

Map 1. The Philippines.

principal ones were Tagalog, Bicol, Ilocano, Ibang, Pangasinan, Pampanga, and Bisaya.[7] In 1902, Governor William H. Taft testified before a US Senate Committee that over 90 percent of Filipinos "speak a language that is confined to a narrow part of the territory of the islands [and it] prevents their communication with the government, with courts, with people from anywhere else except through somebody who speaks their own language and the Spanish language."[8] The Spanish classified Filipinos as Christians or Roman Catholics; non-Christian or pagans, primarily the Negritos; and Moros or Muslims, located primarily in the southern Philippines.[9] Roman Catholic Church records indicated 6.6 million Filipino members were organized into 746 regular parishes, 105 mission parishes, and 116 missions. Only 150 regular parishes had native Filipino rather than Spanish clergy.[10] While the Visayans and Tagalogs clearly formed the majority of the Filipinos, the various groups spoke different dialects, practiced different habits and customs, and during periods of rebellion the Spanish had mobilized some for use against the others. The term Filipino, like that of American, was an inaccurate indicator of a common race, language, or religion.

Discovered by Ferdinand Magellan in 1521 and named after Phillip II—ruler of Spain from 1556 to 1598, the Spanish settled the Philippines in 1565 and established their capital at Cebu on the island of Cebu. In 1571, the capital was moved to Manila, which became the political, military, religious, and economic center of the islands. The Spanish focused on trade and conversion of the Filipinos to the Roman Catholic faith. Spanish officials and military forces remained small in number and closely tied to the clergy—Dominicans, Franciscans, and Augustinians—known as friars. Limited numbers required an indirect Spanish rule that permitted the development of a local ruling class based on land ownership and economic wealth. The Spanish clergy, often the only Spaniards that many Filipinos saw in their lifetime, gained unusual power through governmental and ecclesiastical duties at the local level. Towns consisted of a small center based on a church, government building, and homes of the local elite. By 1898, the Spanish had organized the Philippines into 77 provinces. Barrios or pueblos, outlying smaller communities that were physically separate but administratively a part of the town, surrounded the town center. The Philippines had suffered neglect after Spain's decline following the Seven Years' War.[11] Infrastructure remained basic. Manila and its harbor received limited resources. In the mid-1800s, Cebu, Iloilo, Zamboanga, and Legaspi joined Manila as authorized ports of trade. Coastal trade was permitted between these ports and the numerous islands. Roads were limited; trails were common. Both deteriorated during the rainy season. A single railroad line on Luzon ran north from Manila through the central Luzon plain to the Lingayen Gulf.

As a poor colony, agricultural products provided the mainstay of the Philippine economy. Rice, or palay, served as the chief food and principal crop. Different regions grew hemp or abaca, tobacco, sugar, copra, coffee, coconuts, chocolate, corn, wheat, indigo, sesame, peanuts, cotton, and grasses for fodder. These crops provided food; material and dyes for the local textile industry; oils from coconuts, castor beans, sesame, and peanuts; aromatic plants such as tobacco, coffee, chocolate, nutmeg, betel, cinnamon, and pepper; and grasses for fodder for carabaos,[12] cattle, and horses. Minerals were limited both in quantity and quality. Local industries developed in various regions producing cloth, blankets, mats, and hats. Manila served as the center for the manufacture of cordage, the processing of tobacco, the refining of sugar, and the production of soap.[13] By the late 1800s, abaca, tobacco, and sugar constituted the major Philippine exports. American demand for abaca or hemp, used for ropes and cordage, alternated with the demand for sugar as the primary export.[14]

Filipinos

As with other Spanish colonies, Filipino society consisted primarily of two classes: a small, powerful ruling group and everyone else—the poor, weak, uneducated, and economically dependent. At the top of the ruling class were the Spaniards or *peninsulares* and their Philippine-born descendants or *insulares*. Far below were the non-Spanish native-born Filipinos or *indios*. At the top of the local Filipino elite were local elected leaders or *principales* whose prestige came from political power, owners of large estates or *hacenderos* whose prestige came from economic wealth, and local political bosses or caciques. Local politics consisted of struggles within these groups for control of political patronage and access to economic opportunities. Family ties and business ventures solidified common interests. Society was built on personal relationships reinforced by economic dependence and social respect.[15] A Chinese minority—merchants, artisans, and moneylenders—occupied a central position in the Filipino cash-crop economy at both the provincial and local levels. They constituted a special part of the Filipino elite. Mixed-blood Chinese mestizos frequently owned land, lent money, and received special respect.[16] For the poor, however, a strict patron-client relationship existed. They worked as farm hands, tenant farmers, or day laborers. The quality of their existence—family, social, economic, physical—depended on the relationship with their patron. Social mobility for most Filipinos was minimal.

5

Local leaders did not govern alone. They had to contend with the friars, normally *peninsulares*. Not only did the *principales* have to accept the open contempt that most friars had for Filipinos, but they were also limited by the friars' special duties. The priest represented the church and the colonial government. In fact, the friars were an indispensable component of Spanish colonial rule. The priest was responsible for maintaining census and tax records, for supervising the selection of local officials and police, for reporting on the character and behavior of the natives, for reporting all acts of sedition, for public health measures, and for education. Priests held special powers and proved capable of either assisting or resisting the efforts of leaders.[17]

In the last half of the 19th century, an influential group became prominent. Members of the elite who had received some university education in the Philippines or abroad were known as *ilustrados*. This group embraced liberalism, reform, and greater involvement of Filipinos in the governing of the Philippines. When an 1872 revolt in Cavite was put down, several prominent *ilustrados* were exiled to Guam or the Marianas and three Filipino priests associated with liberal reform were executed. Begun by Filipino students and émigrés in Europe, the Propaganda Movement sought change through reform. Its goals included freedom of speech and association, Spanish and Filipino equality, equal opportunity between Spaniards and Filipinos for government positions, secularization of the clergy, a public school system separate from the clergy, and Philippine representation in the Spanish Parliament.[18]

Jose Rizal, the foremost member of the Propaganda Movement, was a wealthy Chinese mestizo from Laguna province. He began his medical studies in the Philippines, but completed his studies at the University of Madrid. Not just a physician, Rizal was a prominent writer, scholar, and scientist. His two novels—*Noli Me Tangere* or *Touch Me Not* published in 1886 and *El Filibusterismo* or *The Reign of Greed* published in 1891—raised Filipino national consciousness. His books, banned by the clergy, were smuggled into the islands and widely read. Rizal returned to the Philippines in 1892 to resolve a family matter and to continue his reform efforts in the islands. In July, he created the Philippine League, a national, nonviolent, reform association. Spanish reaction was swift, and he was arrested and exiled to the island of Mindanao. In exile, Rizal watched the division of the national movement between *ilustrados* advocating peaceful reform and others advocating revolt and independence.[19]

On 7 July 1892, Andres Bonifacio, a self-educated man without formal power or influence, founded the *Katipunan* or "Highest and Most Honorable Society of the Sons of the Country" in the Tondo district of

Manila. Its goal was independence from Spain. Organized similar to Masonic lodges, the *Katipunan* was a clandestine society with secret passwords, rituals, ranks, and colored hoods. Its members completed their initiation by signing a *pacto de sangre* (blood oath).[20] Appealing primarily to the poverty-stricken and uneducated, by 1896 the *Katipunan* had spread to the provinces around Manila and had grown to 30,000 men and women, mostly Tagalogs. Bonifacio became president of the *Katipunan* on 1 January 1896 and immediately began planning for an armed uprising that was to begin with a massacre of Spanish officials. When an informer told a Spanish friar about the existence of the *Katipunan*, Bonifacio took action.[21]

Fleeing to the hills, Bonifacio issued his *grito de balintawak*[22] or "cry of Balintawak" that called all Filipinos to revolt. The Revolt of 1896 began with Bonifacio's forces attacking Spanish military garrisons in Manila. Bonifacio quickly proved to be a poor military leader; his *Katipunan* forces had few successes against Spanish colonial forces. South of Manila in Cavite province, however, a 27-year-old former municipal captain of mixed Tagalog–Chinese blood from a family of modest landowners near Kawit and a member of the *Katipunan* since 1895, Emilio Aguinaldo y Famy initially defeated local Civil Guard and regular Spanish units. Although Rizal had no ties to the *Katipunan*, Spanish authorities arrested, tried, and executed him on 30 December, thus creating a martyr that inspired the rebels or *insurrectos*. A split between supporters of Bonifacio and Aguinaldo was resolved in March 1897 when Aguinaldo was elected *Katipunan* president and Bonifacio sidelined. Bonifacio withdrew his supporters to create a separate movement, but when fighting broke out between the two factions, Aguinaldo had Bonifacio arrested, tried, and executed on 10 May 1897. By then, persistent Spanish military operations conducted with locally-raised Filipino units from other provinces had destroyed the *insurrecto* capability to conduct conventional operations. Aguinaldo shifted to guerrilla warfare and retreated from Cavite province into the mountains of Bulacan province.[23]

By June 1897, Aguinaldo had established himself at Biyak-na-Bato and issued a proclamation in Tagalog that summarized his political goals: expulsion of the friars and division of their property among the secular clergy; return to the original owners the lands seized by the friars; greater economic and political autonomy; freedom of the press; religious tolerance; and equitable treatment of Filipinos. Independence was not an overt objective. In August, armistice negotiations began with the new Spanish governor. On 14 December 1897, the Pact of Biyak-na-Bato ended the uprising. Aguinaldo, along with 27 companions, was exiled to Hong Kong with a payment of 800,000 Mexican pesos—400,000 paid immediately, 200,000 when 700 firearms were surrendered, and 200,000 after the traditional singing of the Te Deum in Manila that marked the end of an insurrection. A general amnesty was to be declared and 900,000 Mexican pesos were to be paid as indemnity to Filipinos who had suffered damages. Although not specified in the pact, Aguinaldo expected the Spanish governor-general to enact limited reforms. However, he instituted few reforms, declared a general amnesty on 25 January 1898, and paid Aguinaldo his initial 400,000 pesos, with another 200,000 pesos going to *insurrecto* leaders who had remained in the Philippines. On his arrival in Hong Kong on 31 December, Aguinaldo put his money in a bank and waited for a chance to renew the revolution. It came sooner than he could have imagined.[24]

Filipino Revolutionaries or *Insurrectos*

The declaration of war between the United States and Spain on 25 April 1898 and the subsequent sinking of the Spanish fleet in Manila Bay by the American Asiatic Squadron commanded by Commodore George Dewey on 1 May provided the Filipino revolutionaries an unexpected opportunity. American consuls in the region made Dewey aware of the Filipino revolutionaries and a shortage of ground forces caused him to reach out to them. On 19 May, Aguinaldo returned to Cavite, conferred with Dewey, and shortly thereafter accepted the suggestion that he lead a rebellion against the Spanish garrison in Manila. Whether or not Dewey promised independence is uncertain, but he did provide limited arms and plenty of encouragement. "I permitted it as a good military act. The Filipinos were our friends, assisting us; they were doing our work. I believed then that they would be so thankful and delighted to get rid of the Spaniards that they would accept us with open arms," Dewey testified before a Senate Committee in 1902. "I was waiting for troops to arrive, and I felt sure that the closer they [the Filipinos] invested the city the easier it would be when our troops arrived to march in."[25]

While the Americans waited, the Filipino revolutionaries acted. By 24 May 1898, Aguinaldo consolidated his control by declaring himself dictator until power could be handed over to a president and representative body. That day he issued a proclamation to the Filipino people declaring:

> The great North American nation, the cradle of genuine liberty, and therefore the friend of our people, oppressed and enslaved by the tyranny and despotism of its rulers, has come to us manifesting a protection as decisive as it is undoubted disinterested toward our inhabitants, considering us as sufficiently civilized and capable of governing

for ourselves our unfortunate country. In order to maintain this high estimate granted us by the generous North American nation we should abominate all those deeds which tend to lower this opinion, which are pillage, theft, and all sorts of crimes relating to persons or property, with the purpose of avoiding international conflicts during the period of our campaign.[26]

On 27 May 1898, an initial arms shipment paid for by an American consul general arrived—2,282 Remington rifles with ammunition. By the end of May, military operations began with the occupation of Cavite province and the investment of the Spanish garrison in Manila.[27] Not only were the revolutionaries determined to besiege Manila, they planned to establish control over Luzon and the entire archipelago. Luzon, approximately the size of Ohio, was the immediate theater of operations. It held over half of the Filipino population—3.7 million. Different ethnic groups dominated various regions, but the Tagalogs, who lived around Manila and in southern Luzon, constituted the majority of the population on Luzon.[28]

Supported by his comrades from Hong Kong, by Apolinario Mabini—a political advisor, and by others on Luzon, Aguinaldo, building on his military success, began laying the foundation for Filipino civil government. On 12 June 1898, he declared the Philippines independent. Six days later, Aguinaldo established a local governmental structure and defined responsibilities for towns and provinces. He further differentiated their duties from those of the provincial military governors. On 20 June, Aguinaldo issued 45 rules for local elections, the police, the courts, and taxation. Understanding the local nature of Filipino politics, it was not surprising that Aguinaldo and his advisors began at the local level before addressing archipelago-wide issues. Acting as "president of the revolutionary government of the Philippines and general-in-chief of its army," on 23 June Aguinaldo issued a decree written by Mabini that established the structure of the revolutionary government—the executive, the legislative, and the military and civil judiciary.[29] Following up in mid-July, Aguinaldo formed his first cabinet on which Mariano Trias was Secretary of Finance.[30] Well before the first American troops arrived on 30 June, control over most of Luzon had passed from the Spanish colonial authorities to the Filipino revolutionaries.

To mobilize the population in support of the revolutionary government required time, persuasion, and revolutionary discipline. The delayed arrival of the Americans, who were focused on Manila, provided that time. Establishing local governments and issuing proclamations helped persuade, if not establish control. As for discipline, Aguinaldo made clear on 15 July 1898 his determination that the population would support this effort:

> All Filipinos must understand that they are now in the *Katipunan*, whether they want to be or not, and hence it is the duty of all to contribute life and property to the arduous enterprise of freeing the people, and he who disobeys must stand ready to receive the corresponding punishment. We can not free ourselves unless we move united in a single desire, and you must understand that I shall severely punish the man who causes discord and dispute.[31]

Even after Manila fell to the Americans on 13 August 1898, Filipino political organization and control continued to spread. A revolutionary congress with representatives from the provinces convened north of Manila at Malolos on 15 September to draft a constitution and to establish a government for the Philippines. By the end of November, a constitution modeled on that of France, Belgium, and several Latin American countries had been approved. During this period, the struggle between conservatives and radicals about the framework of the government and the policy to be followed with the United States dominated their agenda. Given the outcome with its limitation of franchise to the local elites, the revolutionary government proved, in the end, to be political rather than social in character. When it became clear in early January 1899 that the Americans planned to annex the Philippines, the struggle shifted to those who favored peace against those who favored war. Either way, the revolutionaries promulgated their constitution on 21 January, made Malolos their capital, and announced Aguinaldo as president. Based on attempts to understand American politics from newspaper accounts, the Filipinos placed their hopes in the anti-imperialist movement in the United States. They firmly believed the US Senate would not ratify the peace treaty.[32] For most Filipinos, Aguinaldo's government was viewed as representing their interests and reflecting their society better than the Spanish ever had and better than Americans could.

Raising forces to besiege Manila had been the initial military task. The Spanish unintentionally assisted the revolutionaries in two ways: first, by focusing on the defense of Manila, which left isolated garrisons in the provinces to fall to local forces; and second, by creating a militia under former *Katipunan* members, arming and training those most dedicated to Spanish defeat. Late in May 1898, most of the militia around Manila defected to Aguinaldo and the Tagalog provinces to the south rose in revolt. Some 12,000 to 14,000 Filipinos with Spanish military service eventually formed the core of the revolutionary army. To create an effective military force within the capabilities of Filipino society proved a challenge. Aguinaldo assigned military governors to each province and sent reliable supporters and military forces to consolidate his influence with local leaders.[33] On 20 June 1898, Aguinaldo created both a regular army—soon known as the Army of Liberation—and a revolutionary militia. Militia units varied and included the revolutionary militia or *Sandatahan*, town companies, and units of various sizes raised by local governments or influential persons. He followed on 30 July by having each Tagalog province raise a battalion of provincial troops to augment the three regular regiments that formed the nucleus of the regular army. Although organized along the lines of a modern regular army, the Army of Liberation remained a hodgepodge of units composed of volunteers, *Katipunan* members, Spanish colonial army veterans, and provincial forces whose loyalties lay with their personal commanders. Given its composition, shortage of time, and lack of military experience, the *insurrecto* regular army was ill-trained, poorly armed, and ill-disciplined. The effectiveness of the Army of Liberation would depend on the abilities of its soon-to-be opponent—the US Army.[34]

American Conquest of the Philippines

Sinking the Spanish fleet in Manila Bay and supporting Aguinaldo's Filipinos had not secured Manila, much less the Philippines, for the United States. Following American military tradition, in April 1898 Congress authorized both a volunteer army for the duration of the war to be raised and officered by the states and an expanded Regular Army of 65,000 to fight the Spanish–American War. The initial call went out for 125,000 volunteers. Faced with an unanticipated requirement for troops in the Philippines, the War Department issued a second call in May for an additional 75,000 volunteers. The basic unit was the infantry regiment— 1,350 officers and men organized into three battalions each with four companies of 108 personnel. On 12 May 1898, Major General Wesley Merritt, the second senior general of the US Army, received command of the Philippine expedition that was to be assembled and organized as VIII Corps at San Francisco.[35] The War Department initially planned to provide 5,000 state volunteers. Seeking an understanding of his mission, Merritt wrote President McKinley on 13 May: "I do not yet know whether it your desire to subdue and hold all of the Spanish territory in the islands, or merely seize and hold the capital." He added, "It seems more than probable that we will have so-called insurgents to fight as well as the Spaniards, and upon the work to be accomplished will depend the ultimate strength and composition of the force." McKinley replied on 19 May that the army of occupation had "the two-fold purpose of completing the reduction of Spanish power in that quarter and giving order and security to the islands while in the possession of the United States."[36] One historian summed up Merritt's mission as:

> Go to the Philippines, cooperate with the Navy, defeat the Spanish armed forces there, establish order and the sovereignty of the United States. Advise the Filipinos that the United States aims to protect, not fight them; follow existing laws as far as possible; take over public property, the collection of taxes and customs; open the ports to commerce.[37]

After an exchange with Commanding General of the Army Nelson A. Miles, Merritt's request for 6,000 Regulars and 8,000 volunteers was modified to 13,000 state volunteers and 2,000 Regulars. Little was known about the Philippines or the Spanish forces and time was short. One confidential report from the Military Intelligence Division of the War Department proved to be nothing more that the entry on the Philippine Islands from the *Encyclopedia Britannica*.[38] Despite these and other problems, the mobilization of VIII Corps proved well organized. On 25 May 1898, the first of three VIII Corps contingents sailed from San Francisco.[39]

The first contingent of VIII Corps arrived at Manila on 30 June after stopping on the way to occupy Guam. Merritt arrived with the last contingent on 26 July. He found that roughly 13,000 Spanish soldiers in Manila were besieged by a larger Filipino Army of Liberation—just as Admiral Dewey[40] had hoped. Discussions with Dewey provided Merritt a general understanding of the situation ashore, to include the relationship with America's Filipino partners.[41] Negotiations with Aguinaldo permitted VIII Corps to occupy a sector of the siege lines on 29 July. Given his immediate task of securing Manila, Merritt and others negotiated with Spanish Governor-General Dom Fermin Jaudenes y Alvarez seeking his surrender. Fearful of the Army of Liberation and seeking an honorable solution to his problem, Jaudenes agreed to surrender to the Americans after a sham battle if the Americans promised not to permit the Army of Liberation to enter Manila. Understanding that the Filipinos, who had besieged Manila with American encouragement and little material support for over 3 months, would be outraged, Merritt did not discuss it with them. On 13 August, supported by Dewey's cruisers, VIII Corps attacked and occupied Manila with American losses of 17 killed in action (KIA) and 105 wounded in action (WIA). The next day, Jaudenes surrendered to the Americans. When the Army of Liberation tried to support the American assault by moving into Manila, American soldiers barred their entry. The Filipinos, surprised and confused by American actions, considered this betrayal a "stunning revelation of how little they were valued as allies."[42] It confirmed the concerns of many Filipinos as to just what the American objectives were in the Philippines. A second siege of Manila now occurred with the Army of Liberation surrounding American-occupied Manila. It differed from the first siege in that discussions between the Filipinos and the Americans continued, but a basic mistrust now existed.[43]

Now began a 4-month period of uncertainty—both for the Americans in the Philippines and for the Filipinos. No one knew what the status of the Philippines would be—independence, partial or complete occupation by the Americans, or re-occupation by the Spanish. Aguinaldo's government knew its goal: independence, perhaps after a short period of American supervision. For the Americans, faced with an anti-imperialist movement in the United States and an uncertainty as to what value the Philippines might be 7,000 miles from its west coast, the final decision slowly evolved. In the meantime, things changed in Manila. With a month on the ground and Manila secured, Merritt asked to be relieved. With experience in the Philippines, he found himself a member of the American negotiating team at the peace conference in Paris. A week after his arrival in Manila, 61-year old Major General Elwell S. Otis[44] found himself Commander of VIII Corps, the Department of the Pacific, and the Philippines on 27 August 1898. As a student of military service and the law, Otis brought unusual credentials to this position. Some would denigrate his strict attention to detail, his commanding from Manila, and his reliance on what the Filipinos in Manila told him, but no American commander had faced the civil-military challenges Otis did—far from home and with little guidance. Confined to Manila during this period, the Americans tried to maintain cordial relations with the Filipinos. In the countryside, Aguinaldo's government continued to organize and mobilize the population. Few Filipinos saw an American during this time; most saw representatives of the Aguinaldo government. On 10 December 1898, the Treaty of Paris was signed ceding Cuba, Guam, and Puerto Rico to the United States. In addition, the United States bought the Philippines for $20 million. Eleven days later, President McKinley notified Otis that "the actual occupation and administration of the entire group of the Philippine Islands becomes immediately necessary" and that the military government is to be "extended with all possible dispatch to the whole ceded territory." The task of the US Army in the Philippines was to "win the confidence, respect, and affection of the inhabitants of the Philippines" by proving "the mission of the United States is one of benevolent assimilation, substituting the mild sway of justice and right for arbitrary rule."[45] For Otis, besieged in Manila with 21,000 troops, these instructions exceeded his current capability. However, US Navy control of the seas permitted the movement of troops to the southern Philippines to relieve isolated Spanish garrisons. Although some of Aguinaldo's supporters continued to hold out hope that the US Senate would fail to ratify the treaty,[46] both sides began preparing for war as outbreaks of violence followed by negotiations became a common pattern along the siege lines of Manila.[47]

Unexpectedly, but predictably, war in the Philippines—a war of conquest to Filipinos, an insurrection to Americans—began late in the night of 4 February and into the morning of 5 February 1899. Both sides blamed the other as events spun out of control beginning a 9-month conventional war that would be followed by 31 months of guerrilla warfare. American attacks drove the Army of Liberation from its entrenchments around Manila. Surprisingly, Filipino marksmanship proved poor, offsetting the superiority of its smokeless powder Remington rifles. The American state volunteers were armed with black powder, shorter-range Springfield rifles while the Regulars were armed with smokeless powder Krag-Jorgensen rifles. Few American casualties and 3,000 Filipinos killed demonstrated the American lethality and the Filipino determination to resist. Filipino attempts to negotiate the next day were rejected by Otis. On 10 February 1899, Major General Arthur MacArthur's 2d Division attacked Caloocan, 12 miles north of Manila along the railroad, capturing engines and railway cars (see map 2). A fierce street battle in Manila on 23 February ended Filipino resistance there. The Army of Liberation's hold on Manila was broken. Bloodied but undefeated, it withdrew north of Manila and occupied strong, entrenched positions along the railroad. Aguinaldo made several adjustments to his forces. He appointed Mariano Trias, a Tagalog, to command Filipino forces in southern Luzon and Antonio Luna, an Ilocano, as Chief of Operations for the Army of Liberation operating north of Manila. In addition to reorganizing and centralizing his regular forces, Aguinaldo issued two decentralizing decrees. The first required all men from 16 to 59 years of age to join a local militia and to arm themselves with war bolos. The second established local guerrilla units based on towns and barrios.[48] These attempts to improve the leadership of the Army of Liberation did not address its poor marksmanship, its limited firearms, its defective ammunition, its inability to maneuver, nor its ill-discipline. Luna attempted to bring discipline and subordination to the Army of Liberation, but his methods were ultimately disruptive. To Otis and many American commanders, Aguinaldo and the Tagalogs were the *insurrectos*, not the Filipinos.[49]

14

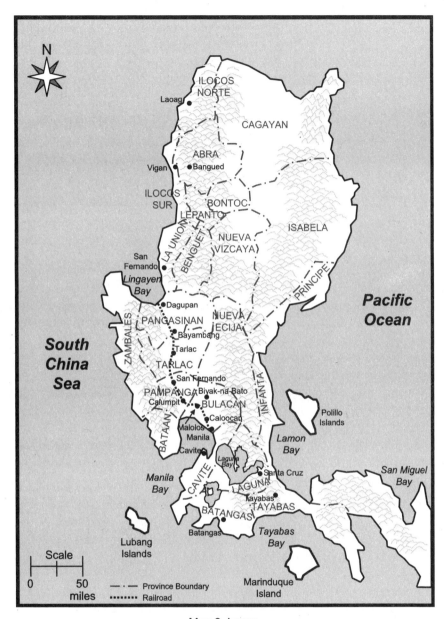

Map 2. Luzon.

Facing threats from the north and south of Manila, Otis reorganized VIII Corps with a two-brigade 1st Division commanded by Major General Henry W. Lawton to defend in the south while MacArthur's three-brigade, 12,000-man 2d Division attacked north along the railroad to capture Malolos, the capital of the Philippine Republic, and to destroy the Army of

15

Liberation. MacArthur attacked on 25 March 1899 and captured Malolos on 31 March. The Army of Liberation suffered a series of defeats, but Luna withdrew each time burning towns as he retreated. MacArthur, in contrast, told his soldiers:

> It is . . . one of the most important duties of American soldiers to assist in establishing friendly relations with the natives by kind and considerate treatment in all matters arising from personal contact. To exasperate individuals or to burn or loot unprotected houses or property is not only criminal in itself, but tends to impede the policy of the Untied States and to defeat the very purpose which the Army is here to accomplish.[50]

Lawton made a limited attack to the south, which convinced Aguinaldo that the next American thrust would be in the southern provinces. Luna then launched a series of attacks on the 2d Division on 10 and 11 April 1899. These were repulsed. After Colonel J. Franklin Bell led the 2d Division scout unit on a reconnaissance that captured a critical bridge turning Luna's position, MacArthur attacked on 24 April. Three days later, Calumpit fell. Final pushes were made on 4 May by MacArthur to San Fernando and to the south by Lawton. By then, the 2d Division had fought 18 major engagements in its 40-mile advance along the railroad with combat losses of 53 KIA and 353 WIA. Its supply lines were a muddle and its units ravaged by illness. Even 1st Division's month-long advance to the south halted because of logistics difficulties. Combat losses were 9 KIA and 35 WIA, and 515 fell to disease. Terrain and weather hindered the American advances as much or more than the *insurrectos*.[51]

Senior American field commanders, along with their state volunteer troops, were eager to press the fight now that war had begun. Otis, on the other hand, had a different perspective. His troops were limited in number; his requirements almost unlimited. The further he advanced, unless he destroyed the Army of Liberation in a single blow, the more troops he required. His state volunteers became eligible for mustering out on 11 April 1899.[52] By mid-April with 26,000 soldiers, Otis could field no more than 16,000 for operations—5,000 garrisoned the Cavite naval base; 5,000 assigned to provost duties in Manila, staff assignments, hospitalized, or imprisoned; and 1,000 occupying relieved Spanish garrisons in the southern Philippines.[53] Logistics proved a challenge. Terrain, absence of maps, disease, and weather became major concerns. By 12 May the 2d Division had 2,160 of its 4,800 soldiers, 45 percent, on sick report.[54] Enemy forces still threatened Manila from both the north and the south.

While American soldiers had shown an ability to attack and take Filipino entrenched positions with few losses, they had not destroyed the Army of Liberation. American commanders found that "climate and terrain, exhaustion, poor logistics, and miscommunication had denied them" what they so desperately sought—"a decisive battle."[55]

During the spring fighting, a three-man Philippine Commission—chaired by Dr. Jacob G. Schurman, President of Cornell University and working for the State Department—arrived on 4 March 1899. Dewey and Otis were to be commission members. Appointed by McKinley before hostilities began, its task was "to facilitate the most humane, pacific, and effective extension of authority throughout these islands, and to secure with the least possible delay, the benefits of a wise and generous protection of life and property to the inhabitants."[56] War now compromised its status. Otis, the governor-general, and Dewey were preoccupied with other matters. Through a series of hearings and contacts with the Filipinos, the Commission sought to understand the aspirations of the Filipinos. It then issued a widely circulated proclamation—printed in English, Spanish, and Tagalog—that became the first formal statement to Filipinos of the general principles by which the United States intended to govern the islands. Filipino leaders in Manila were generally satisfied. Aguinaldo requested a 3-month cease-fire on 28 April to gather the Filipino Congress to discuss peace, but Otis denied it. The Commission opened a dialog with Filipinos that were not hostile to American rule. It widened the split in Aguinaldo's government between those who supported peace and those who supported a war for independence. In frustration, Luna arrested the delegates authorized by the congress, cabinet, and president of the Philippine Republic to meet with the commission. Luna's rift with Aguinaldo ended similar to that of Bonifacio in 1897. Aguinaldo summoned Luna to a meeting on 5 June at which Luna was assassinated. Despite these efforts, Schurman failed to coordinate his work with Otis, much less convince Otis of its importance.[57] At the end of May, Otis telegraphed Secretary of War Russell A. Alger:

> Have attended only few meetings . . . for lack of time. Recommendations . . . unknown to me until called upon to unite in proclamation publishing them. Declined, believing time not opportune. . . . Commission has been beneficial in gaining confidence of leading, well-disposed natives in beneficent intention of United States. Doubt if it has accomplished anything further. . . . Shall be no friction between commission and myself if I can avoid it.[58]

In the small area around Manila under American control, the commissioners agreed with Otis that benevolent pacification was working there. But

Otis's focus remained on the destruction of the Army of Liberation. The Commission concluded in its lengthy report that:

> ... after a careful consideration and study, it was the opinion of the Commission that the Philippine people were not capable of independent self-government, and that independence for which some of them said they were fighting was, in the opinion of the Commission, an ideal at present impossible, not only because of their unfitness for it, but because of their inability to preserve it among the nations even if it were granted.[59]

Marginalized by Otis and Dewey and working without any direct responsibilities, the Commission returned that summer to the United States, published its report, and disbanded.

During the summer of 1899 when a routine report would begin: "Rainy season. Little island campaigning possible in Luzon. . . . 12% sick,"[60] Otis had time to focus on his numerous tasks—maintaining his current positions, rotating state volunteers home, building a new army with their replacements, preparing for a fall campaign to destroy the Army of Liberation, and instituting benevolent pacification measures in Manila and outlying islands. With limited resources, operations had gone well since February. However, by the end of September 1899 the American Army occupied only 120 of the 42,000 square miles of Luzon and controlled a small part of its population. As an American historian observed:

> The Eighth Corps had an unprecedented task, for Americans had never before engaged in a colonial war of conquest. . . . Indian resistance was always on a smaller scale. . . . Once defeated, the Indians could be confined to reservations, but no Philippine reservation system was feasible. For pacification to succeed, the Army had not only to defeat Aguinaldo's army but also to make the Filipinos want American rule or at least tolerate it peacefully. Yet the proper mix between coercion and benevolence was not easily discovered.[61]

Otis tested his initial benevolent assimilation measures through his military government in Manila. He saw his most important task as "simply to keep scrupulous faith with these people and teach them to trust us."[62] Building on experiences from the Indian wars, his policy reflected a benevolent paternalism combined with a firm-but-fair approach. It also reflected a progressive design for social-engineering—"bestow upon a grateful society a host of social, political, and economic reforms to produce a more

18

efficient and honest government and a more modern, rational, and organized society"—that had its foundation in education.[63] Otis tried to attract Filipino leaders who were open to American government by working closely with leaders in Manila. To provide guidance for his units in the more peaceful southern Philippines, on 8 August 1899 Otis issued General Orders 43 that prescribed measures for creating local governments. Basically, local leaders were to be elected by voice vote by members of an open town meeting—a political system perhaps more suitable to New England than to Filipino towns. Commanders and their troops were reminded of their critical role if a policy of attraction was to work.[64]

While benevolent pacification occupied part of his time, Otis also focused on rebuilding his forces in preparation for his fall campaign. The state volunteers began rotating home in May and continued into the summer. Primarily to support operations in the Philippines, on 2 March Congress had authorized the War Department to maintain a Regular Army of 65,000 and a federally raised volunteer force of up to 35,000. The volunteers were to be organized into 25 infantry regiments numbered consecutively beginning with the 26th United States Volunteer (USV) Infantry Regiment. They were to serve until 30 June 1901. The volunteers of 1899 were carefully selected—many were veterans of the Spanish–American War, were well trained and disciplined, and were led by Regular officers selected by the War Department. This conscious design was to combine the best of the state volunteers—aggressive fighting spirit, initiative, adaptability, esprit de corps—with the strengths of the Regulars—discipline, leadership, and training. By mid-August 1899 the 26th USV through 35th USV Infantry were filled, the 36th USV and 37th USV Infantry had been created in the Philippines from state volunteer veterans, and the 11th USV Cavalry was raised. In August the 38th USV through 47th USV Infantry were recruited, followed in September by the Afro-American 48th USV and 49th USV Infantry.[65] By the end of 1899, over half of the American Army in the Philippines would be USV infantry regiments.[66]

To augment American Army strength and to gain information on Filipinos, Otis began in early September to recruit Filipinos to work with American units. The Macabebes, members of a tribe often used by the Spanish to suppress rebellions, had a "reputation for cruelties and excesses when armed for service among their neighbors, and the fears entertained about them on this score were not long afterward realized."[67] They would introduce American soldiers to an interrogation technique known as the "water cure." Lieutenant Matthew A. Batson,[68] 4th Cavalry, organized and trained the 1st Macabebe Scouts, a 110-man company armed with Krag rifles. Formed into four to six man teams, they proved useful as guides, scouts, and in reducing guerrilla attacks on American supply lines. The 2d Macabebe Scouts was organized on 21 September and the 3d Macabebe Scouts on 6 October. By the beginning of the November campaign, VIII Corps had raised its Filipino strength from zero to a five-company battalion commanded by Batson that included a small Filipino–American unit known as Lowe Scouts.[69] Within a year, the scouts would include Tagalogs, Panpangans, and others. These indigenous forces augmented American troop strength that reached 29,000 troops organized into 15 Regular and 8 USV regiments by the end of October.[70]

The Philippine Republic struggled during the summer of 1899 trying to maintain control given its series of demoralizing defeats and its internal struggle with a peace faction that sought negotiation with the Americans. Its power was limited to the reach of its officials and military commanders. The Army of Liberation—demoralized by American victories and racked by faction—numbered 4,000. The June 1899 assassination of Luna, approved by Aguinaldo, did not improve conditions. Aguinaldo focused his efforts to restore the spirit of the Army of Liberation, but the results were meager. The Army, even more than under Luna, remained a collection of units loyal to their commanders who argued with one another as often as they worked together. The officers remained independent and noncooperative. For the Americans, differentiating between the Army of Liberation and guerrilla forces under the command of regional commanders in areas under American control proved difficult.[71]

Otis devised a campaign plan to isolate and destroy the Philippine Republic and its Army of Liberation near Tarlac. As a diversion south of Manila, Brigadier General Theodore Schwan attacked Kawit, the home of Aguinaldo in Cavite province. To the north, MacArthur's 2d Division fixed the Army of Liberation as the plan unfolded. On 9 October 1899, Brigadier General Samuel B.M. Young's Cavalry Brigade led Lawton's 1st Division north along the eastern edge of the central Luzon plain. This movement was to prevent the Army of Liberation from escaping into the mountains of north-central Luzon and to establish a supply line for the 1st Division. A practical concept on paper, it proved impossible to execute as planned. After only a short advance in 4 weeks time, Otis ordered the 2d Division to attack north on 5 November. Two days later, Brigadier General Loyd Wheaton landed on the southeast Lingayen coast to prevent the escape of any remnants of the Army of Liberation north into the Ilocos region of northwest Luzon. On the same day, Young—with a force of 1,100 composed of Macabebes, three troops of the 3d Cavalry, a battalion of the 22d Infantry, and an artillery battery—moved north. Nothing in his previous service had prepared Young for this demanding march through "tropical deluges, mud and water, the swimming, bridging and rafting of innumerable streams most of which were not on the map."[72] The 2d Division quickly overcame the initial resistance by the Army of Liberation and its remnants, to include Aguinaldo, fled to the northeast into the mountains of central and northwest Luzon. Some surrenders occurred. On 23 November MacArthur reported: "The so-called Filipino republic is destroyed. The congress is dissolved. The president of that body is now a prisoner in our hands. The president of the so-called republic is a fugitive, as are all the cabinet officers, excepting one in our hands. . . . The army itself as an organization has disappeared."[73] For the next 3 weeks, Young relentlessly pursued Aguinaldo up the coast into the Ilocos region. Several times Aguinaldo narrowly escaped capture. On 2 December Aguinaldo's rear guard sacrificed itself at Tirad Pass to permit his movement into the mountains of northwest Luzon. Young, with reinforcements from Wheaton, continued north occupying the Ilocano coastal provinces. His units reportedly destroyed the forces of Brigadier General Manuel Tinio, the Tagalog regional commander of the Ilocos region. On 12 December Otis was able to report, "organized rebellion no longer exists, and troops pursuing robber bands. All important and threatened centers of population, north, occupied."[74] With the Army of Liberation and the government of the Philippine Republic seemingly destroyed, Aguinaldo in flight, and northern Luzon undergoing occupation by American forces,[75] Otis decided to clear the Tagalog heartland in southern Luzon.

Just as he planned for the northern campaign, Otis wanted to isolate and destroy the Tagalog forces in southern Luzon by having Lawton's 1st Division, commanded by Lieutenant General Trias, fix the Filipino forces south of Manila in Cavite province. Schwan's brigade moved south along Laguna Bay and then to the west to envelop Trias. On 18 December 1899, in the midst of a typhoon, Lawton was killed in a skirmish at San Mateo. His replacement was Major General John C. Bates. On 4 January 1900 the Americans attacked south into Cavite. Schwan's maneuver was successful, but after initial resistance, Trias's forces had dispersed. Bates' brigades continued south against scattered resistance. By the end of January, American forces overran and occupied the Tagalog provinces of Cavite, Laguna, Batangas, and Tayabas. During the month-long advance, Bates' forces killed 180 insurgents and captured 154 rifles. Schwan's brigade suffered light casualties—six KIA and five WIA.[76] Brigadier General Miguel Malvar, Aguinaldo's commander in Batangas, was reported to have had his unit "annihilated as an organized force." The American officer making this report later commented, "We did not know it then, but the capture of rifles was the important thing, not the scatterment of Filipino organizations."[77] The Tagalog provinces had fallen quicker and easier than the Americans expected.[78]

By the end of January 1900, Otis commanded 63,000 troops—3 cavalry regiments, 17 Regular infantry regiments, and 24 USV infantry regiments—that he could focus on the occupation and pacification of the Philippines.[79] With no large units of *insurrectos* remaining, American troops were "distributed in small detachments and the work of organizing the country for peace was commenced."[80] At the end of March, the War Department dissolved the Department of the Pacific and established the Division of the Philippines commanded by Otis who continued to serve as military governor. Four departments were created within this division: Department of Northern Luzon commanded by MacArthur, Department of Southern Luzon commanded by Bates, Department of the Visayas commanded by Brigadier General Robert P. Hughes, and Department of Mindanao and Jolo commanded by Brigadier General William A. Kobbe.[81] Each department was organized into districts, normally commanded by a brigadier general or colonel. Within each district in Luzon, normally at least a regiment occupied each province. With the war over, Otis focused his forces on benevolent pacification measures—local government, education, public works, and public health—to attract the support of the Filipinos. On the same day the Division of the Philippines was created, Otis issued General Orders 40 with new instructions for organizing local governments. Based on his experience in the Philippines and with the advice of Filipinos in Manila, this general order replaced the 1899 General Orders 43 with a modified version of the 1893 Spanish Maura Law. Franchise was reduced to the *principales* with the result that local governance remained in the hands of the elite.[82] On 23 April, Otis followed with General Orders 58 that established a new judicial code by amending the Spanish code for criminal procedures.[83] Through his efforts at pacification and building on local laws and procedures, many Filipinos in Manila came to view Otis as an honest, fair, and capable administrator. However, security remained an issue. In the last 2 months of 1899, the Americans had fought 229 engagements with the loss of 69 KIA and 302 WIA. The first 4 months of 1900 saw 442 engagements with 130 KIA and 332 WIA. During those 6 months, insurgent losses were 3,200 KIA, 700 WIA, and 2,900 captured.[84] In April, Otis reported that the Division of the Philippines held 116 posts or stations in Filipino towns. Although only half of the estimated 35,000 rifles held by the Filipino insurgents had been captured or surrendered, the security problem appeared normal. Otis stated that "we no longer deal with organized insurrection, but brigandage; to render every town secure against latter would require quarter million men; the war has increased brigandage in Luzon, though it has always prevailed in mountain sections, and in some of the islands much more than it does today."[85] Brigandage had been a chronic problem in the past; it would continue to be a problem that could be handled, but not eliminated. With the war over and pacification under way, Otis requested relief from command.[86]

Secretary of War Elihu Root approved Otis's request. On 5 May 1900, 54-year old MacArthur[87] took command of the Division of the Philippines and assumed the duties of governor-general. Wheaton replaced MacArthur as commander of the Department of Northern Luzon. On his departure from the Philippines, Otis announced:

> I am convinced from observation, investigation, and the expressed opinion of the educated men of the islands that the declared guerrilla warfare will cease within months, and that *ladrone*[88] organizations or robbers in small bands who well know the legal penalties they invite will alone remain to terrorize the people. . . . The American soldier has the inclination and ability to crush it and will be successful.[89]

Published in May by *Leslie's Weekly*, Otis responded to a question about when the war would be over by saying: ". . . the war in the Philippines is already over. . . . Luzon is pacified and there are only a few outlying districts where the natives are still terrified by the ladrones into a show of opposition to us. You will see that there will be no more fighting of any moment. What there is will be but little skirmishes which amount to nothing."[90] Time would tell just how accurate Otis's assessment would be. However, the task of completing the pacification of the Philippines and its transition to civil government would fall on the officers and men under MacArthur's command. To assist him in civil matters, the Secretary of War had appointed the Taft Commission. It would arrive in Manila within days.

Insurrectos Shift to Guerrilla Warfare

Forced to accept the superiority of American forces in conventional operations, Aguinaldo convened a council of war at Bayambang on 12 November 1899 that led to a major change in strategy by the *insurrectos*. The remnants of the Army of Liberation were to disband and return to their provinces. Henceforth, the *insurrectos* would revert to guerrilla warfare. Employed against the Spanish in 1897, guerrilla units had assisted the Army of Liberation against the Americans. This shift required a decentralization and localization of operations. Guerrilla districts were created under a general officer who divided it into zones under the commands of majors or colonels. A local organizational structure with a linkage to local leaders had been created in 1898 when the revolutionary militia was formed and other local forces were required of each town.

The 1887 Spanish regulations provided guidance to the *insurrectos* for conducting guerrilla war. Guerrilla leaders were informed that:

> The object of the guerrillas will be constantly to fight the Yankees in the towns occupied by them, attacking their convoys, inflicting all the injury they can upon their patrols, their spies and their small parties, surprising their detachments, destroying their columns when they pass by places favorable to our attacks, and inflicting exemplary punishment on traitors to prevent the people of the towns from unworthily selling themselves for the gold of the invader; but in addition they will protect the loyal inhabitants and will watch over their property and defend them from bandits and petty thieves.[91]

> The guerrillas should make up for their small numbers by their ceaseless activity and their daring. They shall hide in the woods and in distant barrios and when least expected shall fall upon the enemy. . . . but they shall be careful to never rob their countrymen. We repeat that we must not give or accept combats with such a powerful foe if we have not the greatest chance of success . . . even as should we route him three times or five times, the question of our independence would not be solved. Let us wait for the deadly climate to decimate his files and never forget that our object is only to protract the state of war.[92]

The purpose of guerrilla warfare was not to win the war. It was to drag the war out to "wear the Americans down, relying on disease, terrain, and frustration to demoralize the soldiers."[93] Aguinaldo and his advisers placed their short-term hope on the anti-imperialist movement in the United States and the glowing descriptions of the heroic Philippine resistance in some American newspapers. Having as little understanding of the United States and its political system as Americans had of the Filipino situation, it is understandable that they "not unreasonably, placed undue importance . . . [on] them."[94] Consequently, for Aguinaldo the best case scenario was that Filipino guerrilla warfare, with the resulting American demoralization, would secure a victory of the Democratic candidate and anti-imperialist William Jennings Bryan in the upcoming November 1900 presidential elections. Only time would tell both the accuracy and the wisdom of his strategy.[95]

What Otis and most American commanders saw as routine lawlessness was actually the beginnings of the Filipino version of low scale, organized guerrilla warfare. Even in early 1900 when the Americans became aware of Aguinaldo's decision to go to guerrilla warfare, they failed to understand what it meant, what it looked like, or how it worked. They remained predisposed to view it as a *ladrone* problem. For the US Army this was understandable because:

> ... living among such a large, hostile, and culturally alien people was a new experience. The Indian campaigns were not analogous. In the Philippines the army never had the railroads, buffalo hunters, and the push of white settlement to uproot and degrade their primitive foe. The Indian wars were amateur melees compared with the insurrection waged in 1900.[96]

National figures like MacArthur and Aguinaldo would continue to provide guidance and inspiration, but guerrilla war became close, personal, and local. Filipino guerrilla leaders would come to the fore—Tinio, Malvar, Juan Villamor, Father Gregorio Aglipay, and Juan Cailles—to resist American occupation. How effectively the Americans responded depended on how quickly they understood the nature of the *insurrecto* threat and then on how quickly they developed effective countermeasures. As we will see in the next two chapters, this varied from place to place.

Notes

1.   Graham A. Cosmas, *An Army for Empire: The United States Army in the Spanish–American War* (Shippensburg, PA: White Mane Publishing Company, Inc., 1994), 108–110.

2.   Walter Millis, *The Martial Spirit: A Study of Our War with Spain* (New York, NY: Viking Press, 1965), 340. Secretary of State John Hay's 27 July 1898 letter to Theodore Roosevelt: "It has been a splendid little war; begun with the highest motives, carried on with magnificent intelligence and spirit, favored by that fortune which loves the brave. It is now to be concluded, I hope, with that fine good nature which is, after all, the distinguishing trait of our American character."

3.   During the Philippine War, the term "insurgents" or "*insurrectos*" was given to those resisting American government. It meant rebels. The term was not tied to guerrilla tactics. Filipino *insurrectos* fought conventionally and then switched to guerrilla warfare. Today the term "insurgent" has a different meaning.

4.   Charles B. Elliott, *The Philippines: To the End of the Military Regime* (Indianapolis, IN: Bobbs-Merrill, 1917), 64. Most of the islands—seven-eighths—were smaller than 640 acres. In a 1905 census, only 1,668 islands had been named. Today, most references indicate the Philippines have over 7,100 islands.

5.   War Department, Bureau of Insular Affairs, *A Pronouncing Gazetteer and Geographical Dictionary of the Philippine Islands, United States of America, with Maps, Charts, and Illustrations. Also the Law of Civil Government in the Philippine Islands Passed by Congress and Approved by the President July 1, 1902* (Washington, DC: Government Printing Office, 1902), 1–5, 12–13, 81. Hereafter referred to as WD, BIA. This provides a summary of the information about the Philippines available to American officials in 1902.

6.   US Congress, Senate, *The People of the Philippines. Letter from the Secretary of War Transmitting an Article on the People of the Philippines Compiled in the Division of Insular Affairs of the War Department* (Senate Document 218, 56th Congress, 2d Session, 1901), 19.

7.   WD, BIA, 63–68.

8.   Statement of Governor William H. Taft, 31 January 1902. US Congress, Senate, *Affairs in the Philippine Islands. Hearings before the Committee on the Philippines of the United States Senate* (Senate Document 331, part 1, 57th Congress, 1st Session, 1902), 50.

9.   Elliott, 86–87.

10.   WD, BIA, 69.

11.   Ronald E. Dolan, ed., *Philippines: A Country Study* (Washington, DC: Federal Research Division, Library of Congress, 1991), 5–9.

12.   Filipino name for water buffalo.

13.   WD, BIA, 70–76, 95–96.

14.   Dolan, 10–11.

15.   David J. Silbey, *A War of Frontier and Empire: The Philippine–American War, 1899–1902* (New York, NY: Hill and Wang, 2007), 11; Norman G. Owen, ed., *Compadre Colonialism: Studies on the Philippines under American*

Rule (Ann Arbor, MI: Center for South and Southeast Studies, The University of Michigan, 1971), 1–9.

16. Dolan, 11–12.

17. Ibid., 12–14. In 1898 there were 2,150 schools teaching over 200,000 Filipinos basic skills.

18. Ibid., 17–18.

19. Silbey, 12; Dolan, 18–20.

20. "In the name of the one true God and on my honor I swear to be faithful to the society called *Katipunan* or Complete Union, to defend it to the last drop of my blood, to implicitly obey its orders and to keep its secrets from any and all persons not members of the society. And if I fail in its orders to execute its justice may God punish my soul and may the brothers trample upon my body; in testimony of which I sign with my own blood." Oaths and Form of Initiation of the Society Called *Katipunan* or K.K.K, US National Archives, *History of the Philippine Insurrection against the United States, 1899–1903: and documents relating to the War Department project for publishing the history* (Washington, DC: National Archives, 1968), translated 7 July 1900, roll 4. Microfilm. Hereafter referred to as USNA.

21. David F. Trask, *The War with Spain in 1898* (New York, NY: Macmillan Publishing Company, Inc., 1981), 391–393; Dolan, 20–21.

22. Considered by many Filipinos as the beginning of the Philippine Revolution.

23. Trask, 393–395; Dolan, 20–22.

24. Trask, 395–397.

25. Ibid., 404.

26. Aguinaldo, Proclamation to the Philippine People, 24 May 1898. USNA, roll 1.

27. Trask, 405–407.

28. James H. Blount, *The American Occupation of the Philippines, 1898–1912* (New York, NY: G.P. Putnam's Sons, 1912), 232; WD, BIA, 25–27.

29. Aguinaldo's Proclamation of 18 June 1898, Establishing the Dictatorial Government; Aguinaldo's Instructions Concerning the Management of the Provinces and Towns, 20 June 1898; and Aguinaldo's Proclamation of 23 June 1898, Establishing the Revolutionary Government, USNA, roll 1.

30. Trask, 407.

31. James A. LeRoy, *The Americans in the Philippines: A History of the Conquest and First Years of Occupation with an Introductory Account of the Spanish Rule*, 2 vols. (Boston, MA: The Riverside Press Cambridge, 1914), vol. I, fn., 286.

32. Ibid., vol. I, 280–306. In fact, they were almost right. It was ratified by a margin of one vote on 6 February 1899.

33. Companions of Aguinaldo in Hong Kong, General of Brigade Manuel Tinio was assigned the provinces of Ilocos Norte and Ilocos Sur and General of Brigade Miguel Malvar was assigned Batangas province. List of Officers Commanding Various Districts, 1898. USNA, roll 7.

34. Brian M. Linn, *The Philippine War, 1899–1902* (Lawrence, KS: University of Kansas Press, 2000), 22; Brian M. Linn, *The U.S. Army and Counterinsurgency in the Philippine War, 1899–1902* (Chapel Hill, NC: The University of North Carolina Press, 1989), 13–14; Trask, 405. Linn's *The Philippine War, 1899–1902* is the best book on military operations and *The U.S. Army and Counterinsurgency in the Philippine War, 1899–1902* provides an in-depth look at counterinsurgency operations in four districts in Luzon.

35. For details on the mobilization at San Francisco, see Stephen D. Coats, *Gathering at the Golden Gate: Mobilizing for War in the Philippines, 1898* (Fort Leavenworth, KS: Combat Studies Institute Press, 2006).

36. Trask, 383–384.

37. William T. Sexton, *Soldiers in the Sun: An Adventure in Imperialism* (Freeport, NY: Books for Libraries Press, 1971), 19. This reprint of a 1939 book is one of the better early books on the Philippine War.

38. Brian M. Linn, "Intelligence and Low-intensity Conflict in the Philippine War, 1899–1902," *Intelligence and National Security*, January 1991, 91.

39. For details on this period, see Trask, 369–390; Sexton, 17–25.

40. Dewey was promoted to admiral on 7 May 1898.

41. Dewey had been directed by Secretary of the Navy John D. Long not to ally himself formally with the Filipinos.

42. Linn, *Philippine War*, 8.

43. For details on this period, see Trask, 411–422; Sexton, 30–62; Linn, *Philippine War*, 3–25.

44. Major General Elwell S. Otis graduated from the University of Rochester and Harvard Law School. During the American Civil War, he joined the 140th New York Infantry Regiment in 1862 rising in rank from captain to lieutenant colonel with brevet ranks of colonel and brigadier general. Mustered out in 1864 after a head wound, he was insomnious the rest of his life. He entered the US Army in 1866 as a lieutenant colonel in the 22d Infantry. In 1880, he was promoted to colonel of the 20th Infantry and founded the School of Application for Infantry and Cavalry at Fort Leavenworth, Kansas, where he served 4 years as commandant. After serving as chief of recruiting service from 1890 to 1893, Otis became a brigadier general and commanded the Department of Columbia and Department of Colorado. On 4 May 1898 he was appointed major general of volunteers and assigned to VIII Corps. Thomas F. Burdett, "A New Evaluation of General Otis' Leadership in the Philippines," *Military Review*, January 1975, 79–80.

45. Linn, *Philippine War*, 30.

46. Ironically, the treaty was ratified by one vote on 6 February, just after hostilities commenced.

47. For details on this period, see Trask, 423–472; Sexton, 63–78; Linn, *Philippine War*, 26–64.

48. Linn, *Philippine War*, 58.

49. For details on this period, see Sexton, 79–102; Linn, *Philippine War*, 42–64.

50. Linn, *Philippine War*, 105.

51. For details on this period, see Sexton 103–158; Linn, *Philippine War*, 88–116.

52. The United States and Spain exchanged ratified copies of the peace treaty on 11 April 1899. This formally ended the war and the obligation of the state volunteer regiments in the Philippines.

53. Linn, *Philippine War*, 88–89.

54. Kenneth R. Young, *The General's General: The Life and Times of Arthur MacArthur* (Boulder, CO: Westview Press, 1994), 238.

55. Linn, *Philippine War*, 121.

56. John M. Gates, *Schoolbooks and Krags: The United States Army in the Philippines, 1898–1902* (Westport, CT: Greenwood Press Inc., 1973), 80.

57. Elliott, 473–477.

58. Telegram, Otis to Secretary of War Alger received 29 May 1899, in US Army, Adjutant General's Office, *Correspondence Relating to the War with Spain and Conditions Growing out of the Same Including the Insurrection in the Philippine Islands and the China Relief Expedition, Between the Adjutant-General of the Army and Military Commanders in the United States, Cuba, Porto Rico, China, and the Philippine Islands from April 15, 1898 to July 30, 1902* (Washington, DC: Government Printing Office, 1902), vol. II, 998.

59. Eliott, 475.

60. Telegram, Otis to Adjutant General, received 26 June 1899, US Army, *Correspondence*, vol. II, 1019.

61. Allan R. Millett and Peter Maslowski, *For the Common Defense: A Military History of the United States of America* (New York, NY: The Free Press, 1994), 306.

62. Andrew J. Birtle, *US Army Counterinsurgency and Contingency Operations Doctrine, 1860–1941* (Washington, DC: US Army Center of Military History, 1998), 119.

63. Ibid., 102.

64. For details see Gates, 54–75.

65. Linn, *Philippine War*, 125.

66. For details on this period, see Linn, *Philippine War*, 117–138.

67. LeRoy, vol. II, 123.

68. Edward M. Coffman, "Batson of the Philippine Scouts," *Parameters*, 1977, 68–72.

69. Linn, *Philippine War*, 128.

70. Telegram, Otis to Adjutant General, received 3 November 1899, US Army, *Correspondence*, vol. II, 1093–1094.

71. Linn, *Philippine War*, 136–138.

72. Ibid., 147.

73. John R.M. Taylor, *The Philippine Insurrection Against the United States: A Compilation of Documents with Notes and Introduction, Volume II, May 19, 1898 to July 4, 1902*. vol. II, 12. This is a galley proof of an unpublished War Department manuscript in *History of the Philippine Insurrection against the*

United States, 1899–1903: and documents relating to the War Department project for publishing the history (Washington, DC: National Archives, 1968), roll 9. Microfilm. Hereafter referred to as Taylor, USNA.

74. Telegram, Otis to Adjutant General, received 12 December 1899, US Army, *Correspondence*, vol. II, 1120.

75. For details on this period, see Sexton, 158–220; Linn, *Philippine War*, 139–159.

76. Taylor, USNA, vol. II, 14, roll 9.

77. Linn, *Philippine War*, 165.

78. For details see Glenn A. May, *Battle for Batangas: A Philippine Province at War* (New Haven, CT: Yale University Press, 1991), 91–162; Sexton, 221–231; Linn, *Philippine War*, 160–170.

79. Telegram, Otis to Adjutant General, received 6 February 1900, US Army, *Correspondence*, vol. II, 1142.

80. Elliott, 480.

81. Headquarters of the Army General Orders 38, 29 March 1900, US Army, *Correspondence*, vol. II, 1154–1155.

82. LeRoy, vol. II, 283–286.

83. Ibid., vol. II, 279–282.

84. Young, 252.

85. Telegram, Otis to Secretary of War Root, received 10 April 1900, US Army, *Correspondence*, vol. II, 1159.

86. For details, see Linn, *Philippine War*, 185–204.

87. Major General Arthur MacArthur, born in 1845, joined 24th Wisconsin Infantry at the beginning of the American Civil War, received Medal of Honor for actions at Missionary Ridge, brevet colonel at age 19, studied law after the Civil War; joined 13th Infantry in 1866 as second lieutenant, participated in 1885 Geronimo campaign, lieutenant colonel in 1899, brigadier general volunteers at Manila, major general volunteers commanding 2d Division in Philippines, Commander, Division of the Philippines and Governor-General of the Philippines 1900–1901. For a biography, see Kenneth R. Young, *The General's General: The Life and Times of Arthur MacArthur.*

88. Thieves or outlaws.

89. Taylor, USNA, vol. II, 15, roll 9.

90. Sexton, 237.

91. Taylor, USNA, vol. II, 47, roll 9.

92. Sexton, 239.

93. Linn, "Intelligence," 93.

94. Elliott, 459.

95. For details, see Sexton, 238–240.

96. Allan R. Millett, *The General: Robert L. Bullard and Officership in the United States Army, 1881–1925* (Westport, CT: Greenwood Press, 1975), 137–138.

Chapter 2

Pacification of the Ilocano Provinces: First District, Department of Northern Luzon, 1900–1901

... you will establish civil government in the various towns on your line of march, giving at least one day to each town. ... impress on the President and Council and leading people the necessity of a strong, well-organized Police Force, upon which they must mainly rely for protection. ... See that they understand the necessity of protecting themselves against the small bands of Insurgents and Ladrones. ... It is my desire that you use your best endeavors to facilitate tranquility and the return of the people to their peaceful avocations.

BG Samuel B.M. Young, 20 December 1900[1]

On 18 November 1899, Brigadier General Samuel B.M. Young's cavalry brigade—the remnants of an initial force of 1,100 composed of three troops of the 3d Cavalry, a battalion of the 22d Infantry, a mountain battery, and Macabebes—reached Rosario in southern La Union province in pursuit of Aguinaldo (see map 3). Without specific orders, Young turned north into the Ilocano provinces in search of Aguinaldo and his regional commander, Brigadier General Manuel Tinio. A request for assistance to Brigadier General Loyd Wheaton, who had landed on 7 November at San Fabian on the Lingayen Gulf to block Aguinaldo's retreat to the northeast and who had attacked Tinio's 1,200-man brigade entrenched at San Jacinto on 11 November, was refused as not authorized by orders. Undeterred, Young moved north, brushing aside attempts by Tinio to delay him. On 26 November, Major Peyton C. March's battalion of the 33d United States Volunteer (USV) Infantry caught up with Young who ordered March to move toward Candon to deny Aguinaldo an escape route into the mountains of Abra province through the Tirad Pass. On the same day, Young's executive officer, Lieutenant Colonel James Parker, receiving assistance from the *USS Oregon*, accompanied a 201-man naval landing party ashore at Vigan, governmental center of the Ilocos. Greeted by Ilocanos with cries of "Long live the Americans! Death to the Tagalogs!" Parker thought the war was over. On 2 December, March's battalion destroyed Aguinaldo's rear guard at Tirad Pass, capturing Aguinaldo's family and staff, but failing to capture him. Young halted south of Vigan on 3 December to gather his forces and to make a reconnaissance of the entrenched Tangadan Pass occupied by 700 *insurrectos* commanded by Blas Villamor and his cousin,

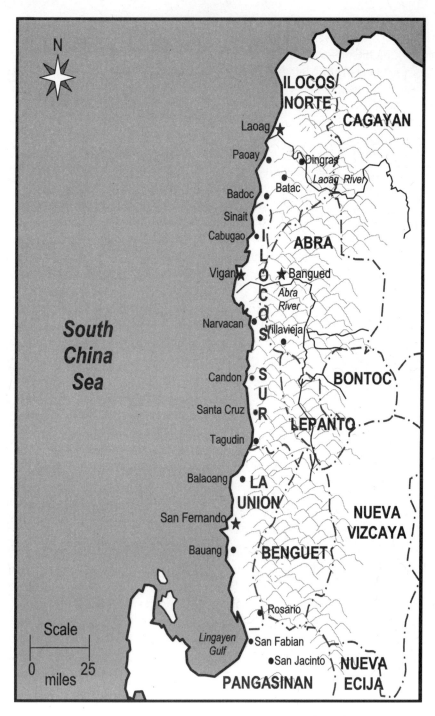

N

ILOCOS
NORTE

CAGAYAN

Laoag

Paoay ●Dingras

Laoag River

Badoc ●Batac

Sinait

Cabugao

ABRA

Vigan ★ ★Bangued

Abra
River

Narvacan ●Villavieja

I
L
O
C
O
S

Candon

BONTOC

Santa Cruz

S
U
R

Tagudin

LEPANTO

Balaoang ● LA
UNION

San Fernando ★

NUEVA
VIZCAYA

Bauang ● BENGUET

South
China
Sea

Rosario

Scale

Lingayen
Gulf ●San Fabian

NUEVA

0   miles   25

●San Jacinto

PANGASINAN

ECIJA

Map 3. The Ilocos in northwest Luzon.

Juan Villamor. Young attacked the next day with 250 soldiers. Fortunately, Colonel Luther Hare, 33d USV Infantry, arrived with 270 men to assist in taking the position. Before dawn on 5 December, Parker, reinforced by 225 soldiers from Major Marcus D. Cronin's battalion of the 33d USV Infantry, was attacked in Vigan by 200 *insurrectos* armed with rifles and war bolos commanded by Jaoquin Alejandrino. A desperate 4-hour fight ensued. By dawn, the *insurrectos* withdrew with heavy losses. Arriving at Vigan the next day, Young directed Hare, with a battalion from both the 33d USV Infantry and the 34th USV Infantry, to pursue and destroy Tinio. Hare moved on two axes into both Abra and Ilocos Norte provinces. The battalion of the 34th USV Infantry, commanded by Lieutenant Colonel Robert L. Howze, found Tinio near Dingras in Ilocos Norte and engaged him in a running battle that ended with the destruction and dispersion of the Tinio Brigade.[2]

In less than a month, Young's forces overran the Ilocano provinces, fought multiple skirmishes, and destroyed or repulsed all resistance. Their focus had been on capturing Aguinaldo and destroying Tinio's units. By mid-December, Young's brigade found itself scattered here and there as the demands of the pursuit had demanded. Many units were worn down—a battalion that started the campaign with over 400 troops finished with 87 men fit for duty. Reinforcements were not available as Major General Elwell S. Otis shifted VIII Corps operations to the southern Tagalog provinces. Fortunately, the initial reception by the Ilocanos appeared friendly. Otis, along with many American officers, believed that resistance would cease when the Americans established local civil government. To pursue this program, on 20 December 1899, Otis assigned Young to command the newly established District of North-Western Luzon. Young's orders, issued that day for the establishment of civil government, were to establish a local government, to explain American expectations as best he could, and then to remain available to provide assistance as necessary. To support pacification of the Ilocano provinces, Young initially had about 3,500 men—3d US Cavalry, 33d USV Infantry, and a battalion from both the 29th USV Infantry and 34th USV Infantry. The American occupation and pacification of the Ilocos was about to begin.[3]

The Ilocos

The Ilocos region, called Samtoy before the Spanish arrived, ran south from the northwest corner of Luzon along the South China Sea coast until it joined the central Luzon plain near the Lingayen Gulf. Mountains comprised 80 percent of the area. The heavily reefed coastline had no all-season harbors. A narrow lowland coastal strip was wedged between the South China Sea and the Gran Cordillera Central or Caraballo Norte mountain range. The coastal strip was rarely wider than 6 miles except in the northern region where in places it reached 12 miles in width. In the north, the Laoag River provided a wide, fertile alluvial plain, and the Abra (gorge in Spanish) River served as the main route into and out of the fertile inland river valleys of central Ilocos. Both were navigable by rafts. The weather could be described as 6 months of drought followed by 6 months of rain. Annual rainfall exceeded 100 inches. The southwest monsoon season precluded maintaining the weekly Manila–Vigan–Aparri postal steamer from June through September. A single wagon road, the Camino Real, ran along the coast connecting the major municipal centers from north to south. In the rainy season, the road deteriorated into a mud track with frequent washouts. A telegraph line ran along the road. Limited interior trails existed. The Ilocos was a harsh, demanding physical environment much of the year.[4]

The Malay settlement of the Philippines began in the Ilocos region. In 1572 when Spanish conquistador Juan de Salcedo arrived, 68,000 heads of families lived in the region. At that time the major towns were Laoag and Vigan, the traditional capital. Salcedo faced stiff resistance from the *indios* before conquering Samtoy. He died from disease in March 1576. The Spanish made Vigan the regional capital. The Ilocanos rebelled against Spanish colonial rule in 1589, 1661, 1762, 1788, and 1807. Each time they failed. Dividing the Ilocos region, the Spanish created Ilocos Norte and Ilocos Sur provinces in 1818. They then created Abra in 1846 and La Union in 1854. The Spanish also organized three mountain districts—Benguet in 1846, Lepanto in 1852, and Bontoc in 1859. The Ilocos remained a loyal, peaceful region until 1898.[5]

With a population of half a million, almost all the inhabitants of the Ilocano provinces lived on the coastal lowlands or in the inland river valleys. Ilocanos comprised almost the entire population. The 1887 Spanish census listed only 15 Chinese and mestizos in Ilocos Norte and several thousand non-Ilocanos in Ilocos Sur—primarily in Vigan, the regional business and governmental center.[6] In 1899, small Chinese communities of 50 in Abra, 320 in Ilocos Sur, and 150 in La Union were reported.[7] In the mountains where the Spanish had left the various tribes ungoverned, the Igorots constituted the major group. In the Ilocos the predominant language was Ilocano. The Ilocos constituted an ethnically, linguistically, and culturally homogeneous region.

Each province was different. Measuring 79 miles north to south and slightly smaller than Rhode Island, Ilocos Norte was the most sparsely settled coastal province. It had greater distance between its towns and villages, particularly north of the Laoag River, than Ilocos Sur or La Union. Located 47 miles by road from Vigan, the capital and largest town, Laoag, had a population of 30,000. To the south of Laoag, the towns of Batac and Badoc supported a combined population of 29,000.[8] Seventy miles long and 21 miles at its widest, Ilocos Sur was less than half the size of Ilocos Norte. With only one-third of its area considered coastal plain, Ilocos Sur had the densest population and largest number of towns and villages. Vigan, its capital, supported a population of 14,200. Its location and harbor with a roadstead made Vigan the economic and governmental center of the Ilocos. Centrally located, Vigan was 47 miles from Laoag and 67 miles from San Fernando by road and 15 miles by river from Bangued. Both Narvacan and Candon were larger than Vigan, with populations exceeding 18,000.[9] La Union was 51 miles north to south and 31 miles east to west. San Fernando, its capital, had an unprotected harbor with two anchorages and a population of 12,900. By road, San Fernando was 67 miles from Vigan and 150 miles from Manila. Unlike the ethnically homogenous northern Ilocano provinces, a Pangasinan minority existed. Balaoang, the second largest town, had a population of 12,200.[10] About the size of Ilocos Norte, Abra was the most mountainous, sparsely settled, and remote Ilocano province. It occupied an area 53 miles north to south and 57 miles east to west. Abra was accessible only by the Abra River, Luzon's third longest river, or by remote mountain trails through passes such as Tarad and Tangadan. Rafting upstream required punting or towing by manpower from its banks. Abra's capital, Bangued, with a population of 16,400 was 15 miles by river from Vigan. Primitive roads connected smaller settlements in the river valleys. Ilocano was spoken in the valleys and Igorot in the mountains of Abra.[11] (See table 1.)

Table 1. 1902 Data on Ilocano Provinces[12]

Province	Ilocos Norte	Ilocos Sur	La Union	Abra
Capital	Laoag	Vigan	San Fernando	Bangued
Area (sq mi)	1,300	490	900	1,500
Population	163,000	186,000	110,000	43,000
Towns / Villages or Hamlets	15 / 119	22 / 587	14 / 240	11 / 68

Agriculture, industry, and trade comprised the Ilocos economy. Agriculture provided the foundation. Although rice was the principal crop, corn, vegetables, sugar cane, peanuts, tobacco, chocolate, pineapples, oranges, lemons, indigo, and cotton were also grown. It was common to raise two crops of rice and corn each year. In Ilocos Norte, Laoag served as the main market place. As a product both for local consumption and for export, raising livestock—cattle, carabaos, horses, and swine—was a principal source of wealth in the coastal provinces. In La Union, the livestock numbered 21,200 carabaos, 8,200 cattle, 5,500 horses, and 2,800 swine. The forests of Ilocos Norte produced the best wood in the Philippines—to include oak and pine—for export to Manila. In the mountains of La Union, sibucao, a valuable dye, grew. Some fishing occurred along the coast. Although the region was poor, food was not a problem. Weaving locally-grown cotton into cloth became a cottage industry for women in Ilocos Norte, Ilocos Sur, and Abra. Few houses lacked a loom. In Ilocos Norte, Paoay enjoyed a reputation for producing "blankets of Ilocos." Copper, iron, gold, and silver were available in the mountains of each province. In Abra, coal was available. In Ilocos Sur, Candon and Narvacan became trading centers with Igorots who worked copper. Most iron products were imported. Vigan and San Fernando were centers for importing European products. Vigan had the only carriage factory in the Ilocos.[13] Eating locally raised foods, dressing in locally-homespun clothing, and living in houses built from locally grown materials, the Ilocanos were "literally self-sufficient in all local needs except iron."[14]

Ilocanos

Like the rest of the Philippines, the Ilocano society was divided into a landed gentry, a very small merchant class, and the poor—the majority. The landed gentry did not own large estates, but they did control daily life and local government through a patron-client relationship among themselves with the elected *principales* and with their tenants. The tax system reinforced the patron-client relationship. Taxes were levied based on *barangay*—a dependence on a particular patron, not on residence. Local government dominated Ilocano politics. Spanish colonial authorities were few in number. Resident *principales* and ex-*presidentes* elected local leaders, in 1900 known as *presidentes* by both the *insurrectos* and the Americans. In most places, this position had been filled by members of a small number of families over the decades. When a *principale* required something to be done, the natural, socially-, economically-, and culturally-driven response was to do it. For the poor Ilocanos, not to do so was unthinkable. Ilocano society was hierarchical, stable, and accepted. Known for their honesty and hard work, Ilocanos disliked other groups, particularly the Tagalogs and Igorots.[15] Like most groups in the Philippines, the Ilocanos were a proud people "quick to avenge insults to personal or family honor, a characteristic which often determined decisions to resist or assist enemy occupation."[16]

The persistent Spanish colonial presence throughout the Ilocos was the local priest, normally a Spanish friar. The ecclesiastical government for the Ilocos was established in Vigan. It was unusual in that both the *peninsulare* friars and the native clergy were Augustinians, but their bishop was from a different order. Beyond ecclesiastical duties, priests participated in local affairs. In addition to the duties required by the Spanish colonial government to maintain the tax rolls, oversee the selection of local leaders, monitor local government, and search out subversives, the clergy oversaw education. The primary purpose of education was to produce pious adults. Primary education, little more than learning to read and write in Spanish or Latin, was to be completed by age 9. Although required by law, public schools seldom existed in the Ilocos. Secondary education, a 5-year course taught by schools recognized by the Bureau of Public Instructions, was followed by an examination administered by a member of the University of Santo Tomas. The only secondary school in the Ilocos was in Vigan. As a minor seminary, it offered only the first 3 years of the 5-year course. To complete a degree, a student had to go to Manila or elsewhere. This restricted secondary education to the *principales*. Often the only local *peninsulare*, the priest had connections in Manila and in Madrid beyond the reach of local leaders, had better education and information about events outside the Philippines, and had duties that brought him into direct conflict with local leaders. Ilocano resentment over the way the clergy interfered in local affairs helped shape events in 1898.[17]

The term "towns" and their population numbers are misleading. A town or *poblacion* consisted of a few houses for the wealthy that were built of carved woodwork with mahogany floors resting on a plastered masonry or brick foundation and roofed with tile. They were located near a church and a public plaza or along a road near open markets. The only building of significance in these towns was the church, a massive brick or stone building with a tile or metal roof and thick walls. Adjoining the church and similarly built was a *convento*, the quarters of the local friar. A more apt description of a town would be a one-street village. The remainder of the population of the town resided in outlying barrios, some located miles away, and lived in wooden, thatched houses made from local, combustible, and renewable materials. Provincial capitals and a few commercial centers had a second residential or business avenue. Only capitals had municipal jails. In towns, prisoners were confined in leg irons and left to be fed by relatives. The only urban center in the Ilocos was Vigan. As the regional Spanish colonial governmental center for centuries, Vigan had grown into a 16-city-block town of cobblestone streets, grand houses, fine churches, schools, government buildings, and warehouses.[18] As such, Vigan became the "political cockpit for all the friar-secular-Spanish-mestizo-*indio* factions of the period."[19]

Considered one of the Philippines most loyal regions in the 19th century, the Ilocanos accepted the Spanish view that the 1896 *Katipunan* uprising was a Tagalog revolt. They responded by providing a squadron of cavalry from Ilocos Norte and 600 infantrymen—300 from Ilocos Sur, 200 from Abra, and 100 from La Union—to the Spanish colonial army fighting against Aguinaldo in 1897.[20] After an inspection tour by Governor-General Primo de Rivera, and in recognition of Ilocano loyalty and support, the Spanish Queen bestowed the title *Muy Noble y Leal* or "Very Noble and Loyal" on Vigan.[21] Despite the absence of Ilocano support for the *Katipunan* rebellion, local mistrust caused the *peninsulare* clergy and Spanish officials in Vigan to seize on the revolt as an opportunity to purge elements of the community. The Ecclesiastical Notary and his representative were arrested and tortured. Because many priests saw the *Katipunan* as a military arm of Masonry, Ilocano Masons, many of them *illustrados*, along with members of the native clergy, found themselves targeted for arrest and torture. Afterward, the friars claimed they had preempted a revolt by their actions; others saw no revolt as an indication that no threat had ever existed. But that would change. The friar's actions caused an Ilocano reaction. Soon thereafter, the *Guardia de Honor*, a lay-based religious sect in La Union, began meeting. On 25 March 1898 in Ilocos Sur, members of the Candon *Katipunan* revolted. Led by Fernando Guirnalda and Isabelo Abaya, it killed several members of the local clergy and declared the establishment of the Republic of Candon. Three days later, Spanish troops arrived, killed most of the rebels, and destroyed the newly declared republic. Guirnalda and Abaya escaped into the mountains not knowing that within months the Ilocos would be freed from Spanish rule.[22]

Manuel Tinio, a Tagalog, returned to his province of Nueva Ecija from Hong Kong in June 1898 to raise a force of *insurrectos* to destroy Spanish rule in the Ilocos. Six months earlier, as a 20-year old general and veteran of the *Katipunan* revolt, he accompanied Aguinaldo into exile. Beginning at San Fernando in La Union in July, Tinio overran the Ilocos from south to north in a 30-day campaign capturing over 3,000 Spanish prisoners. On 13 August, the day the Americans attacked Manila, he entered Vigan. With the surrender of the last Spanish colonial troops in Ilocos Sur shortly thereafter, the Ilocos was freed from Spanish rule after 330 years. The Ilocanos greeted Tinio as a liberator. He established the Tinio Brigade headquarters at Vigan. To oversee the implementation of the civil and military directives of Aguinaldo's government, Tinio created three commands: 1st Zone commanded by Lieutenant Colonel Casimiro Tinio, consisting of La Union and the mountain districts of Beneguet and Amburayan; 2d Zone commanded by Lieutenant Colonel Blas Villamor, consisting of southern Ilocos Sur and Abra provinces and the mountain districts of Lepanto and Bontoc; and 3d Zone commanded by Lieutenant Colonel Irineo Guzman consisting of northern Ilocos Sur and Ilocos Norte provinces.[23] As directed by Aguinaldo, Brigadier General Manuel Tinio spent the next 15 months working with Ilocano local leaders and developing both the Tinio Brigade and the Ilocano militias. When war with the Americans started, Tinio planned the defense of the Ilocos and had 636 entrenchments constructed at critical locations from La Union to Ilocos Norte. When Otis attacked north in the central Luzon plain in the fall of 1899, Tinio left subordinates to secure the Ilocos and moved with 1,200 men into La Union province to assist Aguinaldo escape. What followed was Young's campaign into the Ilocos and the shattering of the Tinio Brigade.[24]

Ilocano *Insurrectos*

Brigadier General Manuel Tinio, the boy general and liberator of the Ilocos, had build a solid civil-military foundation between August 1898 and November 1899, which supported the guerrilla warfare that followed. As Aguinaldo's commander in the Ilocos, he had developed personal ties with Ilocano *presidentes* and had recruited Ilocanos into the Tinio Brigade. Through his zone commanders, he supervised the creation of the *Sandatahan*—the locally recruited, bolo-armed militia. When William B. Wilcox, a US Navy paymaster, visited Vigan in November 1898, he was struck by the youth of Tinio's officers and by what they had accomplished militarily in just a few months—a 3,500-man regular brigade, a militia in every town, and a local defense force in almost every barrio. Although training was considered poor, the Tinio Brigade appeared well armed, supported by a large militia, and widely supported by the Ilocanos.[25] Young's advance into the Ilocos may have scattered Tinio's conventional units, but it did not affect his hold on local leaders and their local militias.

However, tension between Tagalogs and Ilocanos had occurred. Personalities and past events raised questions of trust. Sanctioned by Aguinaldo, the assassination of Antonio Luna, the Ilocano commander of the Army of Liberation, reinforced the general Ilocano mistrust of Tagalogs. Father Gregorio Aglipay, an-excommunicated native priest from Ilocos Norte who had assumed the title Ecclesiastical Governor in the Ilocos when Tinio liberated the region and who had been appointed

Vicar General of the Army of Liberation, accompanied Aguinaldo into the Ilocano provinces during his retreat into the mountains of northwest Luzon. Older than Tinio, a university graduate, an ordained priest, and a proud Ilocano patriot from humble beginnings, Aglipay found it impossible to take orders from the younger Tagalog university dropout. With no formal military commission other than Vicar General, Aglipay assumed the rank of lieutenant general. The personality conflict between Aglipay and Tinio became a public rivalry that continued throughout the insurrection. Unfortunately for the Americans, both shared a determination to resist the American occupation. At times they conferred, but Aglipay conducted guerrilla operations in Ilocos Norte independent of Tinio's control.[26]

Shifting to guerrilla warfare required a reorganization of the Tinio Brigade and a decentralization of operations. In January 1900 Tinio established three units called lines that were commanded by commanders known as *Jefes de Linea*. The commands were the Ilocos Norte–Vigan Line which included Ilocos Norte and Ilocos Sur to south of Vigan; the Abra–Candon Line which included Abra and Ilocos Sur between Vigan and Candon; and the La Union–Santa Cruz Line which included La Union and Ilocos Sur to north of Santa Cruz (see map 4). Each line was divided into companies of 50 to 100 men commanded by *Jefes de Guerrilla*. Unit size depended on available firearms. Ilocos Norte had three companies— not including Aglipay's forces, Ilocos Sur had five companies, La Union had five companies, and Abra had three companies. The companies were numbered sequentially by province. For example, Ilocos Sur had companies Guerrilla Number 1 of Ilocos Sur through Guerrilla Number 5 of Ilocos Sur. In Ilocos Sur, the *Jefe de Linea* of the Ilocos Norte–Vigan Line commanded Guerrilla Numbers 1 and 2 of Ilocos Sur, the *Jefe de Linea* of the Abra–Candon Line commanded Guerrilla Numbers 3 and 4 of Ilocos Sur, and the *Jefe de Linea* of the La Union–Santa Cruz Line commanded Guerrilla Number 5 of Ilocos Sur. The companies were subdivided into *destacamentos* or detachments of 20 men or less. Each full-time guerrilla was armed with a rifle and about 100 rounds of ammunition. Some guerrilla detachments included a limited number of men armed with war bolos.[27] Shortages of firearms and ammunition would plague the guerrillas.

Tinio appointed Lieutenant Colonel Vicente Salazar to command the Ilocos Norte–Vigan Line, Lieutenant Colonel Juan Villamor to command the Abra–Candon Line, and Lieutenant Colonel Juan Gutierrez to command the La Union–Santa Cruz Line.[28] The line commanders had served with Tinio from the beginning. Juan Villamor, whose cousin Blas served as Tinio's executive officer and now worked with Ilocanos on the

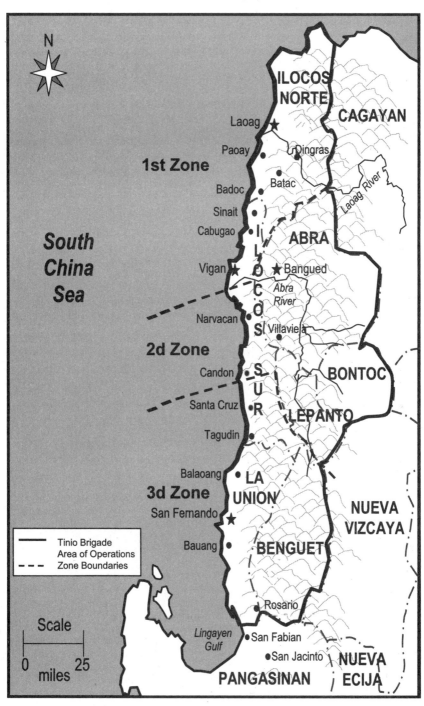

N

ILOCOS
NORTE

CAGAYAN

1st Zone

Laoag
Paoay
Dingras

Badoc
Batac

Sinait

Cabugao

South
China
Sea

Vigan
Bangued

ABRA

Abra
River

Narvacan

Villavieja

2d Zone

Candon

BONTOC

Santa Cruz

LEPANTO

Tagudin

Balaoang

LA
UNION

3d Zone

San Fernando

NUEVA
VIZCAYA

Tinio Brigade
Area of Operations
Zone Boundaries

Bauang

BENGUET

Scale

Rosario

Lingayen
Gulf

San Fabian

0   25
miles

San Jacinto

NUEVA

PANGASINAN

ECIJA

Map 4. Tinio Brigade area of operations.

Abra–Ilocos Sur border, came from an influential extended family in Abra. Born in Abra, Juan Villamor, a former Spanish colonial officer, had been an early advocate of guerrilla warfare. Like Tinio, Gutierrez, a Tagalog, was engaged to a local woman. Major Isabelo Abaya, a leader of the 3-day Candon Republic revolt in 1898 and member of one of Candon's largest families, commanded Guerrilla Number 4 of Ilocos Sur.[29] Most of the company and detachment commanders were members of the Ilocano land-owning class who shared strong family and economic ties and who enjoyed the support of extended Ilocano families. Few had previous military experience, but all commanded because of their local knowledge and influence.[30]

Given the critical role of the population in providing food, supplies, intelligence, and warning to the guerrillas, Tinio understood the key was controlling the *presidentes* and their local government, especially in towns garrisoned by the Americans. Before the Americans arrived, he had organized widespread local militias and emphasized to the *presidentes* the importance of supporting the local militia and nearby guerrilla units. Before the insurrection, local leaders had supported the militia for months with recruits, taxes, food, and supplies. Tinio tried to maintain popular support for resistance to the American occupation through patriotic appeals, through the local patron-client relationships in each town, and even through coercion when necessary.[31] On 20 March 1900 Tinio issued a proclamation as Commander in Chief of Operations in the Region of Ilocos that reminded the population of its responsibilities to support the guerrillas and to resist the American occupation:

> The following will be subject to summary judgment and penalty of death:
>
> 1. All local presidents and other civil authorities of towns and barrios, *rancherias* and other places of their jurisdiction who do not give immediate information to the camps within their jurisdiction at the moment they have information of the movements, plans, directions, and number of the enemy.
>
> 2. Those who, whatever be their age and sex, reveal to the enemy the camp, stopping places, movement and direction of the revolutionary soldiers.
>
> 3. Those who voluntarily offer themselves as guides to the enemy unless it is for the purpose of leading them from the true road.

4. Those who, of their own free will or not, capture revolutionary soldiers without being authorized to do so or who induce them to surrender to the enemy.[32]

The part-time local militia provided not only a reserve for the regular guerrilla units but, more importantly, it provided eyes and ears among the populace. It served as an important tool that could intimidate both by its mere presence and by taking action against traitors. Punishments for informers, designed to punish and to serve as an example for others, ranged from warnings and fines to whippings to death—buried alive, slashed to death by bolo, decapitation by bolo, or thrown alive into a well. Tinio stated, "Although I would regret to have to shed blood of my compatriots, I am disposed to take all the steps necessary to punish rigorously the traitors to the country."[33] A militia in every town and barrio served as an important *insurrecto* instrument of populace control. The militia served as an invisible police force.[34]

After mid-January 1900 Tinio's *insurrectos* fought only as guerrillas. Tinio moved throughout the region inspecting, consulting, encouraging, and commanding his line and company commanders. By June 1900 he established a headquarters at what he called Santa Rosa, a location in the mountains along the Ilocos Sur–Ilocos Norte border north of Sinait in Ilocos Sur.[35] Full-time guerrillas ambushed isolated American units, employed snipers as harassment, and occasionally attacked towns to inflict losses on American soldiers as a reminder to the Americans and to the Ilocanos that the war continued without respite. When attacked by the Americans, the guerrillas would flee to the nearest barrios, hide their weapons, and blend in with the other amigos or friends. Although the militia reinforced the guerrillas on occasion, its primary functions were intelligence, resupply, supporting taxation, and controlling the population. Overlooked by the Americans who searched for the guerrillas, the militia played a critical role in sustaining support for the guerrillas.[36]

Life as a full-time guerrilla was itinerant if not dangerous. Captured records indicated that in April 1900 Guerrilla Number 2 of La Union, commanded by Captain Aniceto Angeles, had 81 members—1 captain, 4 lieutenants, 4 sergeants, 8 noncommissioned officers, 1 bugler, and 63 men. Averaging 24 years of age, the *insurrectos* were all unmarried or widowers. All but two were farmers. They were armed with a mixed collection of 47 rifles, 33 bayonets, and 53 cartridges each. Except for 19 days that no records were found, from 15 August 1900 to 20 April 1901, the unit spent 103 out of 220 days in the mountains patrolling and scouting for Americans between Santa Cruz in southern Ilocos Sur and

Dolores in Abra. It never spent more than 5 nights in the same place. Angeles commanded the Line once when his superiors left to meet with Tinio. Three times he gave up command because of sickness. During those 9 months, the company joined other guerrilla units to attack Americans four times, was attacked by Americans four times, and withdrew ten times when warned by civilian scouts of the approach of American forces.[37] Warnings of American movements were provided by rifle shots, runners, and even the ringing of church bells. Tinio noted that guerrillas were often saved by "the vigilance of the advance outposts which [civilian] . . . laborers make at a good distance from the camps, so that the presence of the enemy is known two or three kilometers away, as well as his direction and sometimes even his number."[38] These poorly armed, small groups of *insurrectos* were the full-time guerrilla adversaries of the Americans.

American Military Operations

In December 1899 Otis divided northern Luzon—30,000 square miles and nearly 2 million Filipinos—into three military districts: north, northwest, and central. To undertake the organization of civil government and to implement the pacification programs, Major General MacArthur commanded 25,000 American soldiers, half of all the forces in the Philippines.[39] A daunting task with so few American troops, yet the destruction of Aguinaldo's Tagalog-dominated revolutionary government and what was viewed as early support of American efforts raised optimistic assessments. Although security remained a problem, it was expected to be resolved by the establishment of local governments with local police forces. On 29 March 1900 the War Department reorganized by creating the Division of the Philippines and the Department of Northern Luzon. The Department of Northern Luzon, headquartered in Manila, was divided into six military districts—First through Sixth.[40] Three weeks later, Major General Wheaton replaced MacArthur who assumed command of the Division of the Philippines on 5 May. In his August annual report, Wheaton's assessment was:

> The natives, other than the Tagalo[g]s, are generally well
> disposed toward the American occupation, and if pro-
> tected will aid in the establishing of such form of self-
> government as they may be able to understand. The mass
> of Tagalo[g]s, when convinced that we are here to stay
> and that the authority of the United States is to be main-
> tained will acquiesce, provided they are protected from
> the men who have dominated them as leaders of the
> insurrection.[41]

The Department of Northern Luzon statistics for the preceding 6 months had been favorable: 41 American KIA, 73 WIA, and 41 missing in action (MIA) or prisoner of war (POW) compared to over 1,000 *insurrectos* KIA and over 1,300 *insurrectos* and 3,400 rifles captured or surrendered.[42]

The Department of North-Western Luzon was reorganized in March as the First District, Department of Northern Luzon. It consisted of 8,000 square miles and half a million people—almost one-quarter of the area and population in the Department of Northern Luzon—in the four Ilocano provinces of Ilocos Norte, Ilocos Sur, La Union, and Abra; and in the three mountain provinces of Benguet, Lepanto, and Bontoc. Other than a small garrison in Benguet, American units were stationed in the more populated Ilocano provinces.[43] Brigadier General Young,[44] a 60-year old cavalry veteran of the American Civil War, the Indian Wars, and the Cuban campaign, commanded First District from Vigan. His outstanding performance in the 1899 fall campaign failed to change the fact that he had been counseled by Otis on his arrival in the Philippines for remarks critical of Otis and that he now served under Wheaton, a former subordinate.[45] Blunt, outspoken, ill-tempered, and distrustful of his superiors, Young was an aggressive commander whose "major contribution to the pacification campaign was his recognition that the guerrilla war was a local war" and who "steadfastly supported his provincial commanders against his superiors and allowed them to develop their own counterinsurgency methods."[46] But that would come later. On 23 January 1900 Young reported, "My belief is that by keeping up a constant hunt after these murderers, thieves and robbers, the country can be cleared within two months."[47]

Young garrisoned the provincial capitals and other towns as problems arose (see map 5). Lieutenant Colonel Howze, headquartered at Laoag, had a battalion of the 34th USV Infantry and two companies from the 12th Infantry to occupy Ilocos Norte. Colonel Hare, 33d USV Infantry, established his headquarters with one battalion at Bangued in Abra. Two battalions were stationed in Ilocos Sur. By March 1900 the 48th USV Infantry, commanded by Colonel William P. Duvall at San Fernando, was responsible for La Union. Troops from the 3d Cavalry worked with the commanders of the coastal provinces. Posts or stations—varying in strength from 50 to 200 in Sinait to 1,000 men at Cabugao in northern Ilocos Sur and Candon in central Ilocos Sur—grew in number from 15 in January to 19 in March to 36 by April. As the number of posts increased, the size of posts shrank.[48] Most American units would remain in the same area through February 1901 conducting a "war of garrison duty, daily patrols, and occasional expeditions."[49] On 1 August 1900 First District troop strength was reported as 3,693—923 in the 3d Cavalry, 583 with Howze in Ilocos

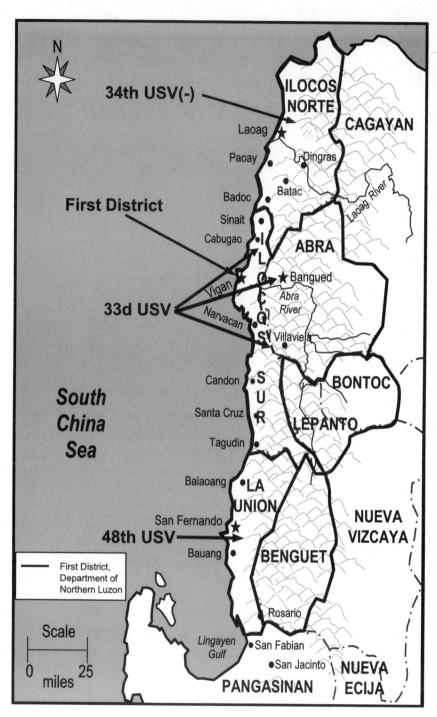

Map 5. First District, Department of Northern Luzon.

Norte, 940 with Hare in Ilocos Sur and Abra, and 1,247 with Duvall in La Union.[50] Low troop strength, lack of intelligence, an unfriendly Ilocano populace, confusion over occupation policies, and the lure of capturing Aguinaldo or Tinio hindered pacification efforts.

Initial Operations

Young was fortunate to have outstanding subordinates who, within their limited resources, pushed Otis's pacification program—establishing civil government, establishing schools, and improving public health. At district headquarters, Captain John G. Ballance, Chief Assistant and Advisor to the Military Governor, coordinated civil governmental and other pacification matters. By April, 63 towns had been organized under General Orders 43 with a *presidente*, a town council, and a police force. By June, 203 schools had 10,700 students, about one-quarter of the possible number of students.[51] Young, a supporter of schools, requested special pay for the soldiers who taught arguing that "the benefits to the government from the knowledge of English that would be acquired by the natives would more than pay the expense."[52] Although increasing numbers were considered progress, basic problems remained. General Orders 43 was flawed. Taxing industry and trades, it was not designed for an agricultural economy. Local leaders and American post commanders had to cross cultural and linguistic barriers to work through an adjustment to duties and responsibilities unfamiliar to both. That took time, understanding, and a willingness by both parties to work together toward a common goal. From the Ilocano perspective, pacification programs "either ignored local customs or were pursued with more self-righteousness than tact." From Young's perspective, the Ilocanos were "densely ignorant and utterly unfit to exercise the right of suffrage."[53] Working across cultural barriers proved no easier in 1900 than it does today.

For the *insurrectos*, hiding from the Americans often in plain sight and supported by the local leadership and the Ilocano populace, intelligence about American movements was excellent. In contrast, American intelligence was limited, at best. Lack of an understanding of Ilocano society, culture, and language, as well as the organization and intent of the guerrilla civil infrastructure, was further compounded by rumors, misinformation, and outright lies. In February 1900, an officer expressed a common American view when he wrote home:

> As a rule the women and children hate the US soldiers and in their language, a kind of dog language, they frequently abuse us. They think we are very ignorant because we don't understand them and because we catch their soldiers

in civilian garb and turn them loose because we can't prove who they are. We cannot have a spy and scouting system because our men are all large and they are small, coppered or brown color, and use an unpublished dog language and will under no circumstance reveal the whereabouts of any of their soldiers.[54]

Young complained on 25 March, "These people are very secretive and as they have no idea of truth, or honor as we understand the word, it is very difficult to find out the truth about anything."[55] Another officer explained, "To us the people were inarticulate; they did not speak Spanish and we could not speak their languages. They were, from secular custom, in the hands of the headmen, whom they obeyed unquestioning."[56] The parole policy compounded American frustration. In May, Young had been informed that crowded prisons in Manila required the parole of all captured *insurrectos* except for officers and others considered most important. Young responded, "I find it very injurious to our cause to release captured prisoners here. They invariably return to the insurgent bands or use their energies in giving aid to them. . . . Those who do not return directly to the mountain bands, act as spies, and disappear finally from our sight."[57] Despite these concerns of Young and others, the parole policy remained in effect: captured *insurrectos* were disarmed and released. Captured ladrones began confessing to being *insurrectos* to avoid punishment for their crimes. It would take a rebellion in Ilocos Norte and an investigation in La Union to provide the Americans a better understanding of the *insurrectos*.

A major threat arose in Ilocos Norte that spring. Howze, the military governor, thought that American policies were working. Laoag's civil government had an active police force. Guerrilla activity, nonexistent for 3 months, permitted his small force to focus on establishing a local government with five infantry companies stationed in five towns. In March 1900 Howze reported a "strong undercurrent of bad spirit and preparations for a revolt."[58] Guerrilla activity increased with convoys attacked, telegraph lines cut, loyal Ilocanos threatened or killed, and reports of Ilocanos being tattooed with *Katipunan* symbols. Rumors persisted that Father Aglipay, working through the local clergy, had formed branches of the *Katipunan* in southern Ilocos Norte. Later, Howze reported that Aglipay had "appealed to the Catholic faith of the natives, calling on them to defend Catholicism against American religion. He is branding men and forcing them to serve him. He is making a great struggle which must be met."[59] When a patrol captured documents on 11 April confirming a planned provincial revolt at the end of April, Howze, with his few troops, acted. On 15 and 16 April, Howze sent detachments into the Badoc-Batac area, the center of Aglipay's support, to disrupt activity by scattering *insurrectos* and inflicting losses. On the night of 16 April, 800 *insurrectos*, using civilians as shields, attacked the 30-man garrison at Batac numerous times in human waves and burned the town. By dawn, *insurrecto* losses were 180 KIA and 135 POW. On the night of 17 April, a similar attack was repulsed in Laoag. In 2 days, Howze's forces had killed over 300 *insurrectos* with losses of 3 KIA and 3 WIA. He reported, "Much of fighting hand to hand by fanatics worked up to a pitch by Padre Aglipay and General Tinio's order. They were regular dervish charges. Slaughter terrible."[60] Howze made a 4-day offer of amnesty which brought in a couple hundred *insurrectos*. When his offer expired, Howze moved directly on Batac where he ravaged the countryside. On 24 April a cavalry troop cornered 300 *insurrectos*, killing 125. Howze's swift defeat of the Ilocos Norte revolt resulted from his prompt, decisive actions. The 520 *insurrecto* dead demoralized the guerrilla movement, undercut its popular support, and exposed its infrastructure.[61] Howze intensified his pacification measures. However, southern Ilocos Norte, particularly the Badoc-Batac area, continued to support Aglipay's *insurrectos* throughout the insurrection.

In First District, La Union province had the most lawlessness in early 1900. When Duvall took command in March, Otis had told him, "This, today, is the worst part of the Philippine islands."[62] No one guessed that when the *presidente* of Bauang turned the leader of the *Guardia de Honor* sect, Crispulo Patajo, over to the Americans as an outlaw, he provided the Americans the key to understanding guerrilla organization in La Union. Interrogated by Lieutenant William T. Johnston, Patajo condemned the *presidente* and offered information about guerrilla units and their relation-ship to the towns that supported and protected them. With this insight into the guerrilla infrastructure, Duvall directed Johnston, assisted by Patajo, to investigate the local governments established by the Americans in La Union province. On 21 May Johnston's report, "Investigation into the Methods Adopted by the Insurgents for Organizing and Maintaining a Guerrilla Force," concluded that despite the destruction of the Army of Liberation, the insurrection was not over and that establishing local gov-ernments alone could not guarantee pacification. In Johnston's words, this was "the first news that the *insurrectos* were actively at work organizing and the first indication that the American authorities had that the native officials of the towns and others were playing a double role."[63] Duvall ordered the destruction of the guerrilla bands and their infrastructure. To accomplish this, Duvall appointed Patajo chief of detectives in La Union and authorized him to recruit an unpaid[64] 400 to 500-man vigilante force raised from the *Guardia de Honor*. Duvall created an intelligence section headed by Johnston to receive information from the *Guardia de Honor*, from surrendered *insurrectos* who received freedom after identifying other *insurrectos*, and from American units. When visits by Blas Villamor and Tinio failed to reduce the influence of the *Guardia de Honor* in La Union province, a bounty was placed on Patajo's head. When the *Guardia de Honor* secured a town, it gave control to loyal vigilantes while American forces swept the countryside for guerrillas. Peasants replaced the *principales*. Rallies provided opportunities for the populace to denounce *insurrectos*, confess misdeeds, embrace the American flag, and join the sect. Once purged, the town remained occupied. Although Duvall ignored Army policy by using what Otis called religious fanatics, Young supported him when inquiries came from Manila. Given an understanding of the local insurgent organization and through the use of a persecuted minority, Duvall had broken the linkage between the guerrillas and the towns and pushed the guerrillas away from the towns. Most of La Union province had been pacified by the end of May 1900.[65]

Shift in Focus: Battle for the Towns

By May 1900 Young had a better understanding of the resistance he confronted and he began to make district-wide changes. Building on the province intelligence section in La Union, Ballance became, in effect, the district intelligence officer. His duties included collecting and distributing military information and administering a network of paid informers. On 22 May First District required all males to have registration certificates. Travel was restricted by a system of passes and reporting procedures. This was followed on 15 June by the publication of portions of General Orders 100 (appendix B) to clarify the laws of war on the classification and treatment of war rebels, war traitors, spies, and prisoners of war. A proclamation prohibiting the provision of food, shelter, or information to the *insurrectos* was followed 10 days later with another prohibiting the possession or hiding of firearms. These two actions clarified to the Ilocanos what was legally permitted and what was not. Post commanders could now hold the guerrillas accountable, as well as the elected leaders and members of the populace who actively supported them.[66] The laws of war, in theory at least, were to be as harsh as the coercion and suasion practiced by the *insurrectos*. A battle for control of the towns began.

Governor-General MacArthur offered amnesty to the *insurrectos* in the Philippines on 21 June 1900. When his offered expired 90 days later, only 5,022 *insurrectos* had surrendered.[67] He took this poor response as an indication that the war was far from over. This reinforced the conclusion of Johnston's report which MacArthur called "altogether the best description which has reached this headquarters of the insurgent method for organizing and maintaining a guerrilla force."[68] MacArthur knew that Aguinaldo hoped that William Jennings Bryan would defeat President McKinley at the polls in November. He also knew that Aguinaldo had, in MacArthur's words, "announced a primal and inflexible principle, to the effect that every native, without any exception, residing within the limits of the archipelago, owed active individual allegiance to the insurgent cause."[69] What he did not know was that on 8 July Aguinaldo ordered general attacks through the archipelago for the nights of 15 and 23 September and an uprising in Manila on 15 September. These attacks were ordered to affect the American presidential election.[70]

At the end of the rainy season, a new roughness began to appear throughout First District, whether from the frustrations of guerrilla war, from assassinations of loyal Ilocanos, or from doing so much with so little. On 16 August Howze notified his commander in Badoc, "I want you to take the most aggressive measures against the natives; clear up that situation even if you have to kill off a large part of the malcontents; do some terrorizing yourself."[71] Telegraph lines always were an easy target for the guerrillas and repair work always risky. In the fall, American reactions became more severe. In August the telegraph poles in La Union province were numbered so that each barrio knew what segment of the line it would be held accountable for if the wire was destroyed. By mid-September, Ilocos Sur commanders were ordered to "shoot all persons who may be found on the road between dark and daybreak, and that wherever the telegraph wire had been cut or pulled down, you cause all houses in the vicinity to be burned to the ground." At the end of September, 3 days after 3 miles of telegraph wire was pulled down between Batac and Badoc, it was reported: "There are no houses or inhabitants within three miles of the road between Batac and Badoc." In mid-October Young ordered, "Shoot anyone you believe to be in any way connected with destruction of telegraph." The next day Wheaton, referring to articles 82 and 84 of General Orders 100, noted, "Armed prowlers by whatever name they may be called . . . cutting the telegraph wire are not entitled to the privileges of prisoners of war."[72] Young supported harsher but legal measures in dealing with the *insurrectos*.

Manned by an understrength battalion of the 33d USV Infantry, Abra had been the most peaceful province in First District. Juan Villamor had used his time to establish a strong link between the guerrillas and the towns. He commanded two 50-man regular companies supported by a local militia with about 150 rifles. American concern began with the July election of officials in Bangued. Out of a population of 13,000, only 26 registered to vote and only 21 voted. March, the military governor, noted "civil government throughout this Province is more or less a farce."[73] When Villamor routed a unit of Native Scouts and killed its American officer on 28 August 1900, things became grim in Abra. Ten days later, Young reported "the insurrection has assumed such proportions in Abra that I do not consider it advisable to send out a detachment with less than one hundred rifles."[74] Conditions continued to deteriorate as supply rafts were ambushed along the Abra River and telegraph wires cut. Although Abra was becoming critical, *insurrecto* attacks had increased throughout First District in September.

In August, Wheaton had forwarded MacArthur a report from a post commander in Ilocos Norte with the remark, "The situation now is this: There are not enough troops in the district to garrison the towns and protect the people who wish to be our friends; the troops are nearly worn out with the amount of work they have had; it is at present out of the question to undertake proper offensive measures. More troops are needed to garrison towns, protect the people, and take proper offensive measures."[75] In early September, Young reported all his provincial commanders independently concluded that the *insurrectos* were working in concert and the common conclusion was that Aguinaldo was the cause. Increased attacks throughout the district required reinforcements. He noted, "To abandon any territory that we are now occupying would be delivering up to insurgent for murder all natives that showed themselves friendly to us. If it is not considered advisable to send all the troops recommended, I request that two regiments be sent here to relieve the strain on the troops of this district, so as to give them rest."[76] Young was concerned, if not alarmed.

Increased *insurrecto* activity prior to the election and the situation in Abra brought reinforcements. From 20 September to 25 October 1900, 17 engagements occurred in First District.[77] On 25 October a 60-man American force attacked over 600 entrenched *insurrectos* commanded by Juan and Blas Villamor. The Americans suffered their worst defeat in First District during the insurrection—5 KIA, 14 WIA, and 8 POWs.[78] From September through November, US losses in First District were 50 percent greater than for the remainder of the pacification period—December 1900 to May 1901.[79] Troop strength increased to 4,900 in October and to 5,900 in November. It was augmented by 250 Native Scouts.[80] By the end of November, the 5th Infantry, commanded by Colonel Richard Comba, occupied Abra with two battalions under orders from Young to "utilize the most severe measures known to the laws of war."[81] With a 50-percent increase in troop strength in 2 months, Young garrisoned additional towns and began aggressive operations throughout the district.

In addition to the battle for towns, a battle for rice began. Many fields lay fallow, not having been planted because of military operations. In addition, three-quarters of the livestock in Ilocos Sur had died.[82] By November First District began to focus on crop destruction in areas of *insurrecto* activity. Crops and foodstuffs—not just buildings—owned by known supporters of the *insurrectos* were destroyed or confiscated. In Ilocos Norte, Howze directed his post commanders to "warn [civic officials] that the feeding, sheltering and harboring of the *Insurrecto* element must at once cease, or the vicinity will be laid to waste, even to the extend of destroying their crops. . . . The most drastic measures will be resorted to in order to put an end to disturbances in this province."[83] Ilocos Norte barrio *presidentes* were also warned that if the presence of *insurrectos* was not "immediately" reported—immediately defined as within 1 hour for each 5 kilometers from the nearest American post—their barrios would be "absolutely destroyed."[84] If the control of the population could not be wrestled from the *insurrectos*, at least the food available could be restricted.

After almost a year of guerrilla warfare designed to wear down American resolve to affect the presidential election, the re-election of President William McKinley on 14 November destroyed the foundation on which Aguinaldo had based his strategy. The Americans would stay, at least for 4 more years. The cumulative effect of intensified pacification programs, increased military actions, harsher measures, and the election demoralized many Ilocanos. Greater numbers cooperated with the Americans. To counter this trend, Aguinaldo informed his followers on 15 November that they had "to learn the verb '*dukutar*' [murder or assassinate] so as to put it immediately in practice."[85] Terror, sustained by killing collaborators, was to become a more prominent role in maintaining the support of local leaders and the population. After a series of murders in Vigan, Young assigned Johnston and Patajo, now the First District chief of detectives, the task of cleansing *insurrecto* influence from the local barrios.[86] When 1,173 bolo men attempted to surrender on 30 November to the post commander at Santa Cruz in Ilocos Sur, the commander, unprepared to care for so many prisoners, asked them to return later. Two days later, 2,180 *insurrectos* surrendered—the largest surrender in First District since 200 had surrendered in April 1900 in response to Howze's amnesty in Ilocos Norte.[87] MacArthur reported to the War Department:

> Two thousand one hundred and eighty Katipunan insurrectos . . . bolo men, came from mountains and surrendered to Gen. Samuel B.M. Young to-day at Santa Maria. [They] renounced insurrection and swore allegiance to the United States. The oath was administered by the padre at the church with impressive religious ceremonies. General

Young attributes the surrender to President's reelection and vigorous prosecution of the war. Although no rifles surrendered, this is important as indicating a reaction among the people of Ilocos Sur. . . . Everything to be pushed as vigorously as possible for the next thirty days.[88]

To discourage surrenders, the first article of Tinio's 21 December proclamation informed his soldiers that any who were guilty of the following would be punished with death:

1. Those who abandon their assigned posts with or without their arms, whether in the field or in barracks.

2. Those who by reason of any dispersion by an accident of war do not present themselves within a period of three days to the detachment nearest to the place where it occurred or to the commanding . . . [official] in the town where he may be located and make an explanation.[89]

Despite Tinio's proclamation, *insurrecto* surrenders continued in the Ilocos throughout the winter of 1900–1901.

December 1900 was a month of change throughout the Philippines. Throughout his command of First District, Young advocated harsher, legal actions against the *insurrectos* and their supporters. Always outspoken, for the first time on 11 December he attacked Army policy as being based on a misunderstanding of the natives and he recommended harsher, European methods. Young believed it was necessary to "inspire rebellious Asiatics, individually and collectively, with a greater fear of the reigning government than they had of the rebels."[90] His 28 December report repeated the theme:

I have been in Indian campaigns when it took over one hundred soldiers to capture each Indian; but the problem here is more difficult on account of the inbred treachery of these people, their great number, and the impossibility of recognizing the actively bad from those only passively so. If it was deemed advisable to pursue the methods of European nations in arms in suppressing rebellions among Asiatics, the insurrection could have been easily put down a month a go. Even now, although the seeds of rebellion have permeated all classes, such methods would soon put an end to all active insurrection.[91]

Young, as directed, explained what he meant by European methods on 17 January 1901.[92] Wheaton's endorsement agreed that the methods

54

described by Young would "speedily end resistance," but that the "vagaries of impracticable public sentiment, which considers war as an affair to be waged for sentimental reasons, will prevent the adoption of many of the ways enlightened nations have found to be necessary in dealing with races that have no idea of gratitude, honor, or the sanctity of an oath, and have a contempt for a government which they do not fear."[93] Young's European methods were not adopted, but MacArthur did undertake a harsher campaign.

MacArthur's Campaign Measures

As governor-general, MacArthur commanded the Division of the Philippines from Manila. Of the 77 provinces that his four departments governed, only 43 were in insurrection; the remaining 34 provinces, 44 percent, remained peaceful.[94] Thus, military and civil matters demanded his attention. The arrival of William H. Taft's Commission in the summer of 1900 had created some jurisdictional issues that the War Department resolved in MacArthur's favor.[95] Working with the governor-general, Taft often suggested harsher measures than MacArthur took. But by December 1900 things had changed. McKinley had been re-elected, American troop strength had reached 69,420,[96] department commanders were recommending harsher measures, and *insurrecto* activities from September to December (see table 2) indicated a weakness that had to be exploited before the USV infantry regiments were shipped home in the spring for discharge on 30 June 1901.[97] The number of *insurrectos* captured and surrendered was up significantly. The engagements initiated by the *insurrectos* were down 50 percent. MacArthur decided to undertake a new, sterner pacification campaign.

Table 2. Division of the Philippines Data on *Insurrectos*,
September to December 1900[98]

September–October	*Insurrectos*	November–December
978	KIA	707
205	WIA	389
613	POW	1,434
54	Surrendered	2,534
424	Arms Captured	486
18	Arms Surrendered	47
52 / 241	Attacks / Engagements	27 / 198

On 19 December MacArthur issued instructions for the campaign to his department commanders convinced that "one of the most effective means of prolonging the struggle, now left in the hands of the insurgent leaders, is the organized system by which supplies and information are sent to them from occupied towns." MacArthur stated the purpose of his campaign was "to interrupt, and if possible, completely destroy this system."[99] Filipinos not actively supporting the Americans were to be considered as enemies and the excuse of fear was no longer acceptable to the Americans. MacArthur stated:

> In carrying out this policy, it is safe to assume that all prominent families, that have not by some public action or declaration committed themselves to American interests, are, either willingly, or under compulsion, engaged in, or at all events, know those, who are employed in this business; and, as a consequence, if not principals themselves, they are accessories to the entire transaction [and] . . . whatever action is necessary the more drastic the application the better, provided only that unnecessary hardships and personal indignities shall not be imposed upon persons arrested, and that the laws of war [General Orders 100] are not violated in . . . the treatment of prisoners."[100]

Active civilian supporters of the *insurrectos* were to be arrested and tried. District commanders were informed of new rules of evidence: "In case it is impossible to find convincing proof that they (peaceful inhabitants) have been assisting the enemy, but there is a suspicion amounting to moral certainty, that such is the case, they will be arrested and a report . . . with recommendations" submitted.[101] Military provost courts could now try civilians and sentence the guilty to punishments ranging from fines to imprisonment. MacArthur's next step was to educate the Filipinos on their duties and responsibilities.

The principal objective of MacArthur's 20 December proclamation to the Filipino people, published in English, Spanish, and Tagalog (appendix C), was "to instruct all classes throughout the archipelago as to the requirements of the laws of war in respect of the particulars herein referred to, and to advise all concerned of the purpose to exact, in the future, precise compliance therewith."[102] Explaining that the rules of law required the population to obey strictly the occupying power in exchange for protection, any hostile actions taken by civilians would make them, by definition, war rebels or war traitors, depending on the nature of their acts. *Insurrectos* that served as guerrillas—unless they were uniformed, formally organized, and full-time serving—lost their legal status as prisoners of war when captured. They, along with war rebels and war traitors, were liable to prosecution for crimes. For the first time, Filipinos were told of their legal status under General Orders 100 and of the clear intent of the Americans to hold them accountable. MacArthur intended that the Filipinos would no longer see American benevolent pacification as weakness.[103] The policy of attraction was to be stiffened by a policy of coercion for those who supported the *insurrectos*.

In his 28 December cable to the War Department, MacArthur summed up his actions and highlighted several issues of concern:

> Progress of pacification apparent to me, but . . . very slow. . . . I have therefore initiated a more rigid policy by issue of proclamation, enjoining precise observance of laws of war, with special reference to sending supplies and information to enemy in field, from towns occupied by our troops, and also warning leaders that intimidation of natives, by kidnapping or assassination, must sooner or later lead to . . . trial for felonious crimes. . . . Would like to emphasize new policy by deporting to Guam at early date a few prominent leaders now in my hands. . . . Pro-American natives Manila, with chief justice at the head, have organized party, which apparently has some elements of cohesion and usefulness. . . . It is difficult to convince people, especially natives, that any of the volunteers will be replaced.[104]

After receiving authorization, on 7 January 1901 MacArthur ordered the deportation of 26 Filipino leaders to Guam.[105] MacArthur then issued orders that captured *insurrectos* would no longer be disarmed, administered an oath of allegiance, and released; they would be imprisoned until the end of hostilities. Only *insurrectos* who voluntarily surrendered would be disarmed, administered an oath, and released.[106] In addition to MacArthur's actions, the establishment of the Federal Party in Manila provided a pro-American Filipino alternative to Aguinaldo. In the first months of 1901, the *federalistas* actively supported American occupation by holding meetings and rallies, by organizing local chapters throughout the archipelago, and by directly contacting guerrilla leaders about surrender.[107] In just 3 months, 250 local chapters were organized with over 150,000 members by June.[108] To offset the anticipated shortfall of troops when the USV regiments departed, MacArthur increased the recruitment of native auxiliaries. He also revived his dormant June 1900 local police program. By mid-June

1901 the native police numbered 6,000; 40 percent had firearms. He increased the Native Scouts from 1,400 on 1 January 1901 to 5,400 by mid-June.[109] During the first half of 1901, MacArthur's subordinates took the war to the *insurrectos* with new tools and a new vigor.

First District Pacification of the Ilocos—Spring 1901

By January First District had about 6,000 personnel—52 infantry companies, 12 troops of cavalry, and 11 companies of Native Scouts—occupying 59 posts.[110] Twelve troops of the 3d Cavalry, commanded by Colonel Wirt Davis, operated in the three coastal provinces. In Ilocos Norte, Colonel L.W.V. Kennon had 10 infantry companies from his 34th USV Infantry, minus a battalion, and 4 cavalry troops. In Ilocos Sur, Colonel Marcus D. Cronin commanded the 33d USV Infantry with 10 infantry companies and 5 cavalry troops; Colonel Duvall remained in La Union with 10 infantry companies and 3 cavalry troops from his 48th USV Infantry and 2 infantry companies in Benguet province; Colonel Comba governed Abra with 19 infantry companies and Lepanto with 1 infantry company from his two battalions of the 5th Infantry and with those of Colonel William R. Groves' 36th USV Infantry. Captain John F. Green commanded 11 companies of the First District Native Scouts.[111] Rotation of volunteer regiments began immediately. The 36th USV Infantry departed for the United States in mid-January, leaving only the 5th Infantry with two battalions in Abra. In February, both the 33d USV Infantry and the 34th USV Infantry departed after being replaced by the 1,256-man 20th Infantry, commanded by Colonel William McCaskey.[112] These forces, most in the field since October, continued to conduct sweeps and local patrols. Columns converged on suspected *insurrecto* locations, but they infrequently met resistance. At most, they usually found only food storehouses, supply caches, or empty camps. However, the cumulative effect of these operations left the guerrillas harried, hungry, sick, and exhausted. The initiative in the field had shifted to Young's forces.

Not only were the guerrilla bands under increased pressure, but in accordance with MacArthur's program, the infrastructure in the towns received special attention. *Federalistas* conducted pro-American rallies and organized chapters in First District towns—in Ilocos Sur the rallies varied in size from 700 to 2,200 participants. Surrenders continued during the first months of 1901 as the support of the insurrection began to weaken. Ilocanos swore oaths of allegiance in ceremonies in which the clergy now played a prominent role. With more pro-American Ilocanos, intelligence about guerrilla bands and its support infrastructure improved. Civilians supporting the *insurrectos* were arrested and tried by provost courts. In January and February 1901 there were more provost court trials in First District than during all of 1900.[113] Cronin, military governor in Ilocos Sur, declared: "My intention has always been to work by pressure upon officials by tracing all insurgent movements, and punishing, through military court, all aiding insurgents even by not notifying us. The officials soon learn that an investigation may be postponed but never abandoned."[114] Veterans with La Union pacification experience brought special skills and insights to other First District provinces. After completing his work in Vigan, Johnston was directed to investigate towns in Ilocos Sur "with a view to breaking up the secret support which had been rendered by these towns to the insurgents."[115] Patajo continued his work as chief of detectives in both Ilocos Sur and Abra provinces. Another La Union veteran conducted a special investigation in Ilocos Norte that produced a census and map of the district, along with information implicating officials in Badoc that permitted the post commander to cleanse the local government by the arrest or dismissal of officials and to destroy the local guerrilla organization by the end of February. Working on the rift between Tinio and Aglipay supporters in Ilocos Norte, officials friendly to Tinio were appointed as *presidentes* in towns supportive of Aglipay.[116] The result was the exposure and arrest of Aglipay supporters. By the time Young relinquished command of First District on 19 February, the linkage between the towns and the guerrillas was being broken and the *insurrectos* in the field were under constant pressure.

Young's replacement, Brigadier General J. Franklin Bell,[117] a 45-year old cavalry officer with extensive Philippine experience, assumed command of First District on 28 February 1901. He arrived in Vigan on 9 March at the conclusion of an inspection tour of La Union and southern Ilocos Sur provinces. Satisfied that Duvall had La Union province under control, Bell had discovered that Ilocos Sur south of Candon had never been garrisoned and the situation there "could hardly be more unfavorable."[118] Concluding that the "only way to prevent insurgents from drawing supplies from [these] towns is to garrison them," Bell immediately created a new subdistrict in southern Ilocos Sur commanded by Major Sedgwick Rice, 48th USV Infantry, whose task was to destroy the local guerrilla forces. Duvall commanded this new subdistrict.[119] With 50 men, Patajo arrived to assist. He recruited an additional 150 men locally, primarily Igorots. Exploiting the antagonism between the Igorots and the *insurrectos*, American units secured the towns while Igorots hunted the *insurrectos*. On 15 April Lieutenant Colonel Juan Gutierrez, commander of the La Union–Santa Cruz Line, was captured by the Igorots. His cooperation with the Americans permitted the pacification of southern Ilocos Sur in just 5 weeks.[120] Bell concluded in his initial assessment on 15 March that "there are now in the district sufficient troops to carry out the same policy pursued in the Third District[121] in the past, and from what I have seen since my arrival here I am convinced more than ever that it is the only policy which will succeed in pacifying the district."[122] Bell continued Young's vigorous pressure on the infrastructure in the towns and on the guerrillas in the field.

Operations by the Villamors in Abra presented Bell his most difficult problem. From 21 March to 7 April, Bell personally inspected Abra, now commanded by Major William C.H. Bowen, 5th Infantry. Bell visited all towns of importance and corresponded directly with the Villamors seeking their surrender. When they refused to surrender, on 9 April Bell forbade all travel and trade into and out of Abra. Then he intensified military operations. Bell had concluded:

> People who have been living under a reign of such abject terror that they have not talked much yet, but when they find that they will be protected, and begin to acquire some confidence in us, we will begin to get more assistance, and all the deviltry which has occurred will begin to unfold itself. For these reasons, I am preparing, and expect to hunt these outlaws like bandits, which they apparently are, without exception; I have given orders that all common soldiers presenting themselves be received kindly, paid for their guns, and released at once, knowing full well if complicity in crimes should be subsequently developed, they can be re-arrested.[123]

To provide forces to accomplish his aim, Bell reinforced Bowen with a battalion of the 7th Infantry on 24 April and five companies from the 48th USV Infantry the next day. Bowen later reported:

> During the insurrection the province suffered severely; every man was either an active insurrector or sympathizer, the consequence being that property had been destroyed right and left; whole villages had been burned, the storehouses and crops had been destroyed, and the entire province was as devoid of food products as was the valley of the Shenandoah after Sheridan's raid during the civil war. The jurisdictions ... of Pilar and Villavieja had been depopulated and this portion of the province had been absolutely destroyed.[124]

Military operations in Abra reached an intensity not experienced in the other Ilocano provinces.

On 25 March Tinio held a council of war in Abra with his subordinate commanders—the Villamors from Abra, Alejandrino from Ilocos Sur, Salazar from Ilocos Norte, and Gutierrez from La Union. Father Aglipay, negotiating with the Americans in Ilocos Norte at the time, did not attend. Although the situation was unfavorable, they agreed that "the final action of the Tinio Brigade should depend upon the decision of the Honorable President [Aguinaldo]."[125] Repeated appeals from *federalistas* and family members, along with the capture of Aguinaldo on 23 March and his 19 April appeal for his followers to accept peace under American occupation eventually had an effect on these guerrilla leaders.

In the meantime, Bell prepared to increase pressure on the *insurrectos* throughout the district. On 12 April he proposed an even harsher action—one rarely used and then only as a local punishment—to his provincial commanders:

> The guerrilla warfare is continued by the substantial aid and comfort given to the insurrectos by the same people whom we are protecting and who are enjoying a certain amount of prosperity due to our magnanimity. They have never felt the full hardship of War and their professions of a desire for peace are merely words and do not come from a full realization of the discomforts and horror of a war that is waged in earnest and with full vigor. It is confidently believed that if the people realize what war is, they will exert themselves to stop the system of aid and contributions to the insurgents by the non-combatants and thus bring hostilities to a close. It is believed that the time has now come to adopt such measures with those so-called 'Amigos' as to cause them to feel the absolute necessity of using their active influences in suppressing the insurrection as well as to stop all possible sources of aid. With that object in view, it is contemplated to cause all the people of the barrios to move into towns with all their supplies and not return to them without written permission from the military authorities. Any person found in the barrios ordered to be abandoned, after ten days' notice, will be treated as insurgents. It is also proposed to have all ports of the district closed. Your views as to the practicality of carrying out each of the above measures in your province is desired. In view of a possibility of a shortage of supplies it is very desirable to have the people bring everything with them.[126]

Two days later orders were issued to evacuate Villavieja in Abra within 10 days or it would be burned to the ground. The inhabitants were granted a 6-day extension on 24 April. On 21 April the barrios of four towns in Ilocos Sur were issued similar orders with a 12-day limit.[127] Before the deadlines arrived, the insurrection in First District ended.

Young's pacification policies, continued and intensified by Bell, culminated in a series of surrenders of major guerrilla leaders during the last week of April. The re-election of McKinley, the creation of pro-American *federalistas*, and the capture of Aguinaldo with his appeal for peace all affected the support of the populace and the resolve of the guerrilla leaders. But it was the constant military pressure on the populace in the towns and on the guerrillas in the field that proved decisive in First District. On 27 April Father Aglipay, after weeks of negotiations, surrendered to McCaskey at Laoag. That same day, the Villamors agreed to surrender to Bowen at Bangued. Three days later Blas and Juan Villamor with 36 officers surrendered and took the oath of allegiance. Tinio sent Bell a letter discussing surrender on 27 April. Bell said Tinio's courier "stated it was difficult for them to get food and very dangerous, all towns being occupied and no food left in barrios; also that the Igorrotes [sic] had turned against them in favor of the Americans."[128] On 30 April Tinio agreed to surrender, and the next day he formally surrendered at Sinait with Alejandrino, Salazar, 25 officers, and 350 riflemen with weapons.[129] On 30 April Bell reported, "The insurrection is now at an end in this district, all the several commands of the insurgents having surrendered."[130] Bell suspended hostilities throughout the district on 1 May to permit the remaining *insurrectos* to surrender peacefully. No fighting occurred after that day. Bell decided not to prosecute any of the guerrilla leaders for their wartime activities and encouraged their participation in the American occupational government. First District American total casualties after 1 March had been one WIA.[131]

The final pacification of First District had been 17 months in the making. It was one of the most difficult yet most complete in the Philippines. Young, supporting and supported by capable regimental commanders, conducted an effective campaign that has been described as "far less centralized than it was regionalized."[132] Assisted by Native Scouts, Patajo's men, Igorot tribesmen, and local police, the First District's final campaign that began in the fall of 1900 had been, by the standards of the day, legal, "harsh, but . . . effective."[133] Young laid the foundation, provided a decentralized command climate, obtained reinforcements, and, by the time of his departure in February, had seized the initiative from the *insurrectos* in the towns and in the mountains. Once in command, Bell "was willing and able to escalate the war to a level that the revolutionary leaders found intolerable, and once they surrendered, he was able to reconcile them to American rule."[134]

Situation in the Philippines, July 1901

By 1 April 1901 MacArthur believed that "the insurrection was rapidly approaching complete collapse."[135] Aguinaldo had been captured and *insurrectos* were surrendering in increasing numbers throughout the archipelago. From less than 500 *insurrectos* surrendering in all the Philippines during the last quarter of 1900, the numbers increased to 900 in January, 750 in February, 7,000 in March, over 6,000 in April, and remained between 1,000 and 2,000 through July. The firearms surrendered followed a similar trend—August to December 1900 less than 200, January and February 1901 a total of 1,800, March to May over 7,500. By April contacts with *insurrectos* had dropped to less than a third of that in early 1901.[136] In addition, important guerrilla leaders were surrendering.

The impact of the Federal Party in reaching out to guerrilla leaders to surrender and to work peacefully with the Americans was important. The first major surrender occurred 15 March when Lieutenant General Mariano Trias, Aguinaldo's commander in southern Luzon, surrendered to the 4th Infantry in Cavite province. Two weeks later he addressed a letter to his former comrades encouraging their surrender. The capture of Aguinaldo in mid-March and the publication of his April peace appeal increased surrenders. MacArthur had added to the beginning of Aguinaldo's statement: "In order to signalize such an important step in the pacification of the country, 1,000 prisoners will, upon taking the oath of allegiance, be released and sent to their homes."[137] Upon Tinio's surrender, Bell forwarded a message from Tinio to Aguinaldo. "After having read your proclamation, and observed the situation and the desires of the Ilocano people, I have thought it convenient to give up my arms. By so doing, I believe I do my duty as a soldier and a citizen."[138] MacArthur ordered the release of another 1,000 prisoners. When two prominent guerrilla leaders surrendered in northern Luzon, MacArthur released an additional 500 prisoners. The last major leader to surrender was Brigadier General Juan Cailles in Laguna province of southern Luzon. Cailles surrendered at Santa Cruz on 24 June with 600 men and 386 rifles.[139] On 21 June MacArthur issued a general amnesty to all *insurrectos*.

As his term as governor-general of the Philippines and commanding general of the Division of the Philippines came to an end, MacArthur stated in June: "The armed insurrection is almost entirely suppressed. At the present writing there is no embodied rebel force in all [North] Luzon. . . . In the

Department of Southern Luzon, disorders still continue in several provinces but in such progressively diminishing force as to encourage the hope that all will be pacified at an early date."[140] During his tenure, American forces had fought 1,026 engagements with *insurrectos*. The results of those contacts and his campaign begun in December 1900 are shown in table 3. With the departure of the USV infantry regiments, the troop strength assigned to the Philippines on 30 June was down to 42,169 of which 5,573 were serving in the China Relief Expedition. With the surrender of the major *insurrecto* leaders and their men, the level of violence throughout the archipelago dropped dramatically. In February the Taft Commission had authorized the establishment of provincial governments with civilian governors elected by the inhabitants. By July, 22 provinces had civil governors and 55 still had military governors. However, those 22 provinces contained almost 50 percent of the population.[141] On 4 July 1901 when William H. Taft assumed duties as Governor of the Philippines and 59-year old Major General Adna R. Chaffee[142] assumed command of the Division of the Philippines, the Philippines were deemed ready for civil government, not military law. Less than 2 weeks later, on 17 July, continued violence in Batangas province on southern Luzon and on the islands of Cebu and Bohol caused military control to be reinstated in those places.[143] The Philippine insurrection was not finished.

Table 3. Division of the Philippines Statistics, 30 June 1901[144]

American	Division of the Philippines 5 May 1900–30 June 1901	Insurrectos
245	KIA	3,854
490	WIA	1,193
118	POW	6,572
20	MIA / Surrendered	23,095
424	Arms Captured	4,871
18	Arms Surrendered	10,822

Notes

1. William H. Scott, *Ilocano Responses to American Aggression 1900–1901* (Quezon City, PI: New Day Publishers, 1986), 25–26.

2. Orlina A. Ochosa, *The Tinio Brigade: Anti-American Resistance in the Ilocos Provinces, 1899–1901* (Quezon City, PI: New Day Publishers, 1989), 77–93; Brian M. Linn, *The Philippine War, 1899–1902* (Lawrence, KS: University of Kansas Press, 2000), 150–159.

3. Brian M. Linn, *The U.S. Army and Counterinsurgency in the Philippine War, 1899–1902* (Chapel Hill, NC: The University of North Carolina Press, 1989), 32–33.

4. Linn, *U.S. Army*, 30; Scott, 1–5; Ochosa, 1.

5. Ochosa, 1–4.

6. Scott, 6.

7. F.G. Verea, *Guide for the Americans in the Philippines*, translated by F.C. Fisher (Manila: n.p., 1899), 103, 119, 137.

8. War Department, Bureau of Insular Affairs, *A Pronouncing Gazetteer and Geographical Dictionary of the Philippine Islands, United States of America, with Maps, Charts, and Illustrations. Also the Law of Civil Government in the Philippine Islands Passed by Congress and Approved by the President July 1, 1902* (Washington, DC: Government Printing Office, 1902), 537–540. Hereafter referred to as WD, BIA; Scott, 5; Verea, 117–118.

9. WD, BIA, 541–543; Scott, 5; Verea, 119–120.

10. WD, BIA, 906–907; Verea, 137–138.

11. WD, BIA, 267–269, Verea, 103.

12. WD, BIA, 267–269, 537–539, 541–543, 906–907.

13. Scott, 5–6; WD, BIA, 269, 540, 543–544, 908.

14. Scott, 7.

15. Ibid., 5–10.

16. Ibid., 6.

17. Ibid., 9–12.

18. Ibid., 7–9.

19. Ibid., 8.

20. Ochosa, 7.

21. Scott, 15.

22. Ochosa, 10; Scott, 13–16.

23. Ochosa, 33.

24. Ochosa, 18–39, Scott, 17–22.

25. Linn, *U.S. Army*, 31.

26. Scott, 20–21.

27. Ochosa, 108–109.

28. Scott, 64.

29. Linn, *U.S. Army*, 39.

30. Brian M. Linn, "Provincial Pacification in the Philippines, 1900–1901: The First District Department of Northern Luzon," *Military Affairs,* April 1987, 63.

31. Linn, *U.S. Army*, 37.

32. Proclamation of Manuel Tinio, 20 March 1900, *History of the Philippine Insurrection against the United States, 1899–1903: and documents relating to the War Department project for publishing the history* (Washington, DC: National Archives, 1968), roll 8. Microfilm. Hereafter referred to as USNA.

33. Scott, 57.

34. Linn, *U.S. Army*, 40.

35. Scott, 60.

36. Linn, *U.S. Army*, 40–41.

37. Scott, 45–47.

38. Ibid., 52.

39. Linn, *Philippine War*, 255.

40. WD, BIA, 138.

41. Quoted in Linn, *Philippine War*, 256–257.

42. Linn, *Philippine War*, 257.

43. Linn, *U.S. Army*, 30.

44. Brigadier General Samuel Baldwin Marks Young, born in Pennsylvania in 1840, private 12th Pennsylvania Infantry 1861, captain 4th Pennsylvania Cavalry 1861, colonel 1864, brevet brigadier general 1865, second lieutenant 12th Infantry 1866, captain 8th Cavalry 1866, service on southwest frontier 1866–79, 3 brevets for gallantry and meritorious service, member organizing faculty School of Application of Infantry and Cavalry 1882, major 3d Cavalry 1883, lieutenant colonel 4th Cavalry 1892, colonel 3d Cavalry 1897, brigadier general 1898, major general volunteers Cuba 1898, brigadier general brigade and district commander Philippines 1899–1901, promoted to major general in February 1901.

45. Linn, *U.S. Army*, 33–34.

46. Linn, "Provincial Pacification in the Philippines," 64.

47. Scott, 26–27.

48. Ibid., 29.

49. Brian M. Linn, "Pacification in Northwestern Luzon: An American Regiment in the Philippine–American War, 1899–1901," *Pilipinas,* December 1982, 15.

50. Report, First District, Department of Northern Luzon, 30 April 1901, in War Department, *Annual Report of Major General Arthur MacArthur, United States Army, Commanding, Division of the Philippines, Military Governor in the Philippine Island* (Manila, PI, 1901), Appendix A, 4–5. Hereafter referred to as WD, *Annual Report MacArthur.*

51. Linn, *U.S. Army*, 33–34.

52. Scott, 39.

53. Linn, *U.S. Army*, 36.

54. Quoted in Brian M. Linn, "Intelligence and Low-intensity Conflict in the Philippine War, 1899–1902," *Intelligence and National Security,* January 1991, 95.

55. Quoted in Scott, 69.

56. John R.M. Taylor, *The Philippine Insurrection Against the United*

States: A Compilation of Documents with Notes and Introduction, Volume II, May 19, 1898 to July 4, 1902, vol. II, 28. This is a galley proof of an unpublished War Department manuscript in *History of the Philippine Insurrection against the United States, 1899–1903: and documents relating to the War Department project for publishing the history* (Washington, DC: National Archives, 1968), roll 9. Microfilm. Hereafter referred to as Taylor, USNA.

57. Quoted in Scott, 58.

58. Linn, *U.S. Army*, 47.

59. Ibid., 48.

60. Ibid., 49.

61. Linn, *U.S. Army*, 45–46; Linn, "Provincial Pacification in the Philippines," 64–65.

62. Linn, *U.S. Army,* 43.

63. Ibid., 44.

64. They received 30 pesos reward for each weapon captured.

65. Linn, *U.S. Army*, 41–45; Linn, "Provincial Pacification in the Philippines," 64.

66. Linn, *U.S. Army*, 49–50.

67. Taylor, USNA, vol. II, 16, roll 8.

68. John M. Gates, *Schoolbooks and Krags: The United States Army in the Philippines, 1898–1902* (Westport, CT: Greenwood Press Inc., 1973), 195.

69. WD, *Annual Report MacArthur*, vol. I, 4.

70. Taylor, USNA, vol. II, 31, roll 8.

71. Scott, 29.

72. Ibid., 31.

73. Linn, *U.S. Army*, 53.

74. Ibid.

75. *Facts About the Filipinos*, USNA, 12–13, roll 8.

76. Ibid., 17, roll 8.

77. Linn, "Pacification in Northwest Luzon," 17.

78. Linn, *U.S. Army*, 53; Scott, 193.

79. Linn, *U.S. Army*, 52.

80. Ibid., 54.

81. Linn, "Provincial Pacification in the Philippines," 65.

82. Scott, 162.

83. Linn, *U.S. Army*, 58.

84. Scott, 33.

85. Taylor, USNA, vol. II, 35.

86. Quoted in Linn, *U.S. Army*, 54.

87. Scott, 161.

88. Telegram, MacArthur to Adjutant General, received 3 December 1900, in US Army, Adjutant General's Office, *Correspondence Relating to the War with Spain and Conditions Growing out of the Same Including the Insurrection in the Philippine Islands and the China Relief Expedition, Between the Adjutant-General of the Army and Military Commanders in the United States, Cuba, Porto*

Rico, China, and the Philippine Islands from April 15, 1898 to July 30, 1902 (Washington, DC: Government Printing Office, 1902), vol. II, 1232.

89. Quoted in Scott, 99.

90. Linn, *U.S. Army*, 53–54.

91. Quoted in *Facts About the Filipinos*, USNA, 47, roll 8.

92. *Facts About the Filipinos*, USNA, 48–49, roll 8. Young's explanation of what he meant by European methods was received by the War Department on 18 March 1901. Young thought Europeans had: 1. Given military commanders supreme authority in a rebellious country, with full power to suspend or change all laws, appoint all officers, and have full control of all receipts and expenditure of money. 2. Full censorship of the press, and removed from the country any press agent whose presence was deemed harmful. 3. Recognized that Asiatics have no idea of gratitude, honor, or the sanctity of an oath, and in all dealings with them to treat them accordingly. 4. Recognized that they were fighting a people the mass of who were worse than ordinary savages, and were not entitled to the benefits of G.O. 100, A.C.O. 1863. 5. Inspired rebellious Asiatics, individually and collectively, with a greater fear of the reigning government than they had of the rebels. 6. Retaliated in kind on their rebellious subjects for every murder and assassination of person because of their being friendly to the reigning government. 7. Authorized the military commander to punish by death summarily or by means of drumhead court-martial, provost or summary courts, all spies, murderers, assassins, and persons caught with arms after having taken the oath of allegiance. 8. Deported all persons caught with arms in their hands, all leaders, civil or military, whose presence in the rebellious country was deemed prejudicial to the permanent sovereignty of the reigning power. 9. Confiscated all real and personal property of every insurgent and their aiders and abettors. 10. Divided the rebellious country into zones, concentrating the people of each zone into circumscribed places, and placed them under absolute military control. 11. Laid waste the country used as hiding-places and rendezvous for insurgents, their aiders and abettors. 12. Appointed only residents of the reigning country to judicial and other high positions in the rebellious country. 13. Given the preference to honorably discharged soldiers, who were competent, in appointment to all positions. 14. Made the military commander the judge, that the condition in any part of the country rendered it available to establish civil government.

93. *Facts About the Filipinos*, USNA, 50, roll 8.

94. Linn, *Philippine War*, 185.

95. Rowland T. Berthoff, "Taft and MacArthur, 1900–1901: A Study in Civil-Military Relations," *World Politics,* January 1953, 196–213.

96. Taylor, USNA, vol. II, 22, roll 9.

97. War Department notified MacArthur on 11 December 1900 that the USV regiments would depart.

98. *Facts About the Filipinos*, USNA, 28, roll 8.

99. Quoted in *Facts About the Filipinos*, USNA, 38, roll 8.

100. Ibid., 39.

101. Ibid., 39.

102. Ibid., 36.

103. Gates, 208.

104. Telegram, MacArthur to Adjutant General, received 25 December 1901, US Army, *Correspondence*, vol. II, 1237–1238.

105. Taylor, USNA, vol. II, 20, roll 9.

106. WD, *Annual Report MacArthur*, vol. I, 16.

107. Linn, *U.S. Army*, 53–54.

108. Gates, 229.

109. Ibid., 213–214.

110. Scott, 29.

111. Ochosa, 199.

112. Report, First District, Department of Northern Luzon, 30 April 1901, in WD, *Annual Report MacArthur*, Appendix A, 15, 18.

113. Linn, *U.S. Army*, 55.

114. Quoted in Linn, *U.S. Army*, 56.

115. Linn, *U.S. Army*, 55.

116. Ibid., 56.

117. Brigadier General James Franklin Bell, born in Kentucky in 1856, West Point graduate 1878, second lieutenant 9th Cavalry 1878, transferred 7th Cavalry 1878, served Fort Buford 1882–86, professor of military science and tactics at Southern Illinois University 1886–89, studied law and admitted to bar, first lieutenant 1890, adjutant 7th Cavalry at Fort Riley 1891–94, aide commander Department of California 1894–97, Fort Apache 1897–98, major of volunteers and engineer officer to VIII Corps 1898, Department of the Pacific chief of military information 1898, captain 1899, major of volunteers 1899 and acting judge advocate 2d Division, colonel of volunteers and commander 36th USV July 1899, Medal of Honor September 1899, brigadier general volunteers December 1899, commanded 4th Brigade of 2d Division 1900, provost marshal of Manila 1900–1901, promoted captain to brigadier general February 1901, commanded 2d District Department of Northern Luzon February 1901, commanded Third Separate Brigade Department of Luzon November 1901–02, commandant Army Service Schools at Fort Leavenworth 1902–06, major general 1907, US Army chief of staff 1906–10, died on Active Duty in 1919.

118. Report, First District, Department of Northern Luzon, 30 April 1901, in WD, *Annual Report MacArthur*, Appendix A, 18.

119. Quoted in Ochosa, 202.

120. Linn, *U.S. Army*, 60.

121. Strict measures employed in central Luzon by Brigadier General "Hell-Roaring" Jacob H. Smith.

122. Quoted in Ochosa, 204.

123. Report, First District, Department of Northern Luzon, 30 April 1901, in WD, *Annual Report MacArthur*, Appendix A, 23.

124. Quoted in Linn, *U.S. Army*, 60.

125. Ochosa, 207.

126. Quoted in Scott, 143.

127. Ibid., 144.

128. Report, First District, Department of Northern Luzon, 30 April 1901, in WD, *Annual Report MacArthur*, Appendix A, 28.

129. Ochosa, 211.

130. Report, First District, Department of Northern Luzon, 30 April 1901, in WD, *Annual Report MacArthur*, Appendix A, 30.

131. Linn, "Provincial Pacification in the Philippines," 65.

132. Linn, *U.S. Army*, 61.

133. Linn, "Provincial Pacification in the Philippines," 65.

134. Linn, *U.S. Army*, 59.

135. WD, *Annual Report MacArthur*, vol. I, 30.

136. Gates, 230–231.

137. *Facts About the Filipinos*, USNA, 103, roll 8.

138. Ibid., 107.

139. Ibid., 113.

140. William T. Sexton, *Soldiers in the Sun: An Adventure in Imperialism* (Freeport, NY: Books for Libraries Press, 1971), 267.

141. Ibid., 266–267.

142. Major General Adna R. Chaffee born in Ohio in 1842, enlisted 6th Cavalry 1861, sergeant 1862, first sergeant September 1862, second lieutenant 1863, twice wounded, brevet captain, first lieutenant 1865, captain 1867, Indian Wars 1867–94, brevet major 1868, brevet lieutenant colonel 1882, major 9th Cavalry 1888, instructor Infantry and Cavalry School at Fort Leavenworth 1894–96, lieutenant colonel 3d Cavalry 1897, commandant Cavalry School at Fort Riley 1897–98, brigadier general volunteers 1898, major general volunteers July 1898, brigade commander Santiago Cuba, chief of staff to governor of Cuba 1898–1900, colonel 8th Cavalry, commander American contingent of relief force during Boxer Rebellion in China 1900–1901, promoted colonel to major general 1901, commander Philippines July 1901–October 1902.

143. Act No. 173, 17 July 1901, in Statement of Governor William H. Taft, 31 January 1902. US Congress, Senate, *Affairs in the Philippine Islands. Hearings before the Committee on the Philippines of the United States Senate* (Senate Document 331, part 1, 57th Congress, 1st Session, 1902), 130–131.

144. WD, *Annual Report MacArthur*, vol I, 21.

Chapter 3

Pacification of the Tagalog Provinces: Second District, Department of Southern Luzon/Third Separate Brigade, Department of North Philippines, 1900–1902

The trouble . . . is not our lack of military power exerted against a foe that will face us, on any terms they might choose. The great problem is to meet and overcome the foe that will not, as a foe, face us. The strength of the latter should not be underestimated. It is a very powerful foe in a military sense: that is, it wears out our troops chasing a phantom, for, even when parties of armed insurrectos are certainly and definitely located, the facility with which they can perform the chameleon act, by throwing away their arms under the bushes or grass . . . and blandly greeting us as good amigos, utterly defeats our best trained and most skillfully conducted operations, or at least that is likely to be the result, and generally it is so. . . . They still have the same appreciation of their incapacity to meet its military power, but they have learned what they did not know, that it can be evaded, and how this can be done. I say this with profound regret.

Colonel William E. Birkhimer, 22 October 1900[1]

On 4 January 1900 Major General John C. Bates' 8,000-man 1st Division attacked south from Manila to conquer the Tagalog provinces of southwestern Luzon. The 1st Brigade, commanded by Brigadier General Loyd Wheaton, consisted of four regiments—4th Infantry, 28th United States Volunteer (USV) Infantry, 38th USV Infantry, and 45th USV Infantry—with cavalry and artillery detachments. Its task was to fix the forces of Lieutenant General Mariano Trias, Aguinaldo's commander in southern Luzon, in Cavite province. The 2,500-man 2d Brigade, commanded by Brigadier General Theodore Schwan, had the 30th USV Infantry and 46th USV Infantry, nine troops of cavalry, two companies of Macabebe scouts, and artillery and engineer detachments. Its task was to move south along Laguna Bay and then turn to the west to encircle Trias's *insurrectos*. The 37th USV Infantry and 39th USV Infantry were the division reserve. Two days into Schwan's movement, Wheaton's 28th USV Infantry attacked south and within 48 hours had scattered the *insurrectos* in Cavite who, instead of continuing to fight as expected, dispersed into hiding. When Schwan completed his envelopment, the *insurrectos* were gone. With the rapid conquest of Cavite, Bates ordered 2d Brigade to Batangas and Laguna provinces and the 39th USV Infantry, reinforced by a 37th USV Infantry battalion, to move to Batangas to capture Santo Tomas, the headquarters of Brigadier General Miguel Malvar (see map 6). On 9 January the 39th USV Infantry fought a sharp engagement with less than 1,000 of Malvar's *insurrectos* at an entrenched position along a river near Santo Tomas, killing 24 and capturing 60 *insurrectos*. Joined by Schwan's 38th USV Infantry, the 39th USV Infantry continued south through Lipa to Rosario freeing 170 Spanish prisoners and capturing 20,000 pesos, gaining some notoriety in the process. On 12 January Bates reorganized assigning Wheaton the 46th USV Infantry and responsibility for Batangas province west of Lake Taal and providing Schwan the 38th USV Infantry and 39th USV Infantry and responsibility for Batangas east of Lake Taal. 1st and 2d Brigade units linked up on 19 January to defeat a 1,000-man entrenched *insurrecto* force at Taal. After eastern Batangas was overrun, Schwan turned 2d Brigade east to Tayabas province and then north to Laguna province. By early February, the heartland of the Tagalog rebellion had been conquered by the 1st Division.[2]

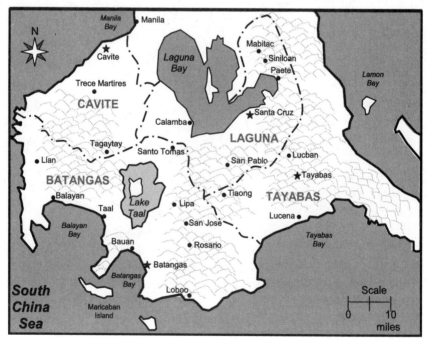

Map 6. Tagalog provinces in southwestern Luzon.

The campaign had been quicker, easier, and less costly than anticipated. In a month's time, all *insurrecto* units that fought had been defeated and seemingly destroyed. 1st Division overran Cavite, Batangas, Laguna, and Tayabas provinces. With the military campaign won, American units occupied towns to begin the transition to local civil government. Unlike in the Ilocos, the initial reception by the Tagalog population was unfriendly, if not hostile. For the Americans in the five infantry regiments—28th USV, 30th USV, 37th USV, 38th USV, and 39th USV—that occupied Batangas, Laguna, and Tayabas provinces, "it would soon become apparent that occupation and pacification were very different problems."[3]

Tagalog Provinces—Batangas, Laguna, and Tayabas

Excluding the peninsula of southern Tayabas province, the heart of this Tagalog area in southwestern Luzon was approximately 70 miles east to west and 35 miles north to south. It consisted of 4,200 square miles. To the north were the mountains in southwestern Cavite province and Laguna Bay; to the east was the Pacific Ocean; to the south were the Balayan, Batangas, and Tayabas Bays; and to the west was the South China Sea. Batangas and Tayabas had good seaports. Located in the center of Batangas province was Lake Taal, an 18-by-13-mile lake with an active volcano in its center. The entire region was generally rugged with numerous ravines, canyons, rivers, and streams. It became mountainous in Batangas west of Lake Taal, in southeast Batangas, in the region along the provincial boundaries, and in eastern Tayabas. Areas along the coasts, on the southern shore of Laguna Bay, and east of Lake Taal in Batangas supported agriculture. Old military roads and telegraph lines along the southern shore of Laguna Bay and east of Lake Taal into southern Batangas and Tayabas connected the provincial capitals. In Batangas province, Rosario and Lipa were important road junctions connecting with the other provinces. Although it rained throughout the year in the mountains to the east, the region experienced a dry season from mid-November to April. The military roads generally sustained loaded wagons in the rainy season, while local roads between towns often deteriorated.[4] Chronic diseases—malaria, small pox, typhoid fever, dysentery, measles, to name but a few—made this region among the unhealthiest in the world.[5] The physical geography made this difficult terrain in which to conduct counterguerrilla operations.

Settled originally by Malays who arrived from Borneo, the region was one of the first on Luzon to be developed by the Spanish after their arrival in the 1750s. The provinces of Batangas, Laguna, and Tayabas were established in the mid-18th century. The population of these three provinces was almost 600,000 by the time of the American occupation. The Tagalogs were the largest ethnic group on Luzon. Tagalog was the predominate language; Spanish was spoken by an educated minority, and along the Pacific Ocean coast in eastern Tayabas, Bicol was spoken.[6] A small Chinese merchant class existed. Even more than the Ilocos, the provinces were ethnically, linguistically, culturally, and politically one in their support for the insurrection.

Each province differed from the others. With its 1,110 square miles, Batangas province was about half the size of Delaware. It had a population three times that of Tayabas and almost twice that of Laguna. Two-thirds of the population lived south and east of Lake Taal. The town of Batangas, a seaport provincial capital with a population of 35,500, was 33 miles by road from Calamba on Laguna Bay to its north and 59 miles from Manila. Lipa, the largest and wealthiest town, had a population of 43,000. Taal, the original Malay settlement and an early Spanish town on Balayan Bay, had a population of 22,000. Laguna formed a U-shaped 750-square mile province along the southern coast of Laguna Bay. Located on Laguna Bay, Santa Cruz, the provincial capital with a population of 13,000, was 47 miles by road from the town of Batangas and 52 miles from Manila. San Pablo, the biggest Laguna town with 19,000 inhabitants, was an important road center. Tayabas, the largest province with 2,300 square miles, was roughly the size of Delaware. Located at an important road center, the town of Tayabas, the capital and largest town, had a population of 16,000. It was 39 miles from the town of Batangas and 7 miles from Lucban, the second largest town with 13,000 inhabitants. Each province was accessible by road. Batangas and Tayabas provinces were accessible by sea and Laguna by Laguna Bay[7] (see table 4).

Table 4. 1902 Data on Second District Provinces[8]

Province	Batangas	Laguna	Tayabas
Capital	Batangas	Santa Cruz	Tayabas
Area (sq mi)	1,110	750	2,300
Population	312,000	170,000	110,000
Towns / Villages or Hamlets	22 / 727	33 / 415	23 / 430

As part of the provinces called by one American commander the "most thickly settled and richest in southern Luzon,"[9] the economy of the region was primarily agricultural and supplemented by fishing and some cottage industry. Rice, sugar cane, coffee, hemp, corn, chocolate, coconuts, tobacco, indigo, and vegetables were grown. Common fruits included mangos, bananas, oranges, lemons, and pineapples. Laguna province, known as the garden of the Philippines, had a climate and soil that permitted it to grow every tropical plant and tree known in the archipelago. Batangas was one of the most fertile and well-cultivated provinces in the archipelago. Coffee had been a major export from Batangas until insects and parasitic fungi attacked the coffee plants in 1889. Coffee production dropped from 6.5 million kilograms in 1888 to 1.4 million in 1892 and was replaced by sugar as the major cash crop.[10] Raising livestock—horses, cattle, carabaos, sheep, and goats—was widespread, particularly in Batangas and Laguna which had 147,000 and 45,000 head of livestock, respectively. Surrounded by the sea and Laguna Bay, fishing provided additional food for many inhabitants. All three provinces produced lumber for local building and furniture needs, even the least forested Laguna. Tayabas province exported some lumber. Weaving was the major cottage industry. Most women had looms in their homes where they wove cloth from silk, cotton, and hemp. Extracting oil from coconuts was another cottage industry in Laguna and Tayabas provinces, and in Laguna province they made bolos. This fertile region produced food in excess of its needs and provided the basic materials required for housing and clothing its inhabitants.[11]

Tagalogs

Like the rest of the Philippines, society in these provinces was divided between the few that had and the many that had not. In wealthy Batangas, the economic elite comprised less than 3 percent of the population.[12] It consisted primarily of owners of large parcels of land and of successful merchants. Most had completed secondary school. In 1891, Batangas had seven 5-year secondary schools. Many secondary school graduates—92 by 1896—attended university in Manila.[13] A few even studied in Europe. The economic elite in Batangas, Hispanicized and Spanish speaking, made their fortunes from coffee and sugar. An American officer described Lipa in Batangas, a town of 40,000 that had about a dozen millionaires at one time, as "about the richest, most enlightened and best blooded town in the islands." Defined by a 9-mile by 10-mile rectangle, the town consisted of 45 barrios. Five families owned three-quarters of the land outside the city limits.[14] At the time, the town of Batangas, the principal port of Batangas, had over 30 men wealthy enough to own a 2,000 peso home; Lipa, by comparison, had 54.[15] This wealth, education, and refinement made it "almost unbelievable" to one historian that "a large segment of the American press would portray Filipinos as uniformly backward and benighted and the Philippine economy as uniformly stagnant and under-developed."[16] Perhaps the press saw the overwhelming majority, not this minority.

As throughout the Philippines, local political power rested in the hands of the current *presidente* or mayor and the municipal council. Selection was not a simple process. The *principales*—current and past town officials—were eligible to vote for the *presidente* and the council. They were often not the economic elite and vice versa. In 1892 in the Batangas town of Santo Tomas, only 85 *principales*—52 current and 33 former officials—were eligible to vote from a population of 10,000. From those eligible, only 13 were allowed to vote: the incumbent and 12 *principales* chosen by lot—6 from those currently serving and 6 from those who had served. Factions of the wealthy, parish priests, and others of local influence who used persuasion and other well-known means to advance their interests lobbied the voters. After the vote, a list was prepared for the Spanish governor-general in Manila that specified three names for *presidente*: the person who received the highest number of votes, the candidate with the second highest vote, and the incumbent. Then the 13 voters elected 4 members for the municipal council. A list of elected council members was also sent to the governor-general for approval. After months of delay in which the governor-general investigated the candidates, he would announce his selection. It appeared that the person with the most votes usually was confirmed. But a result of this process was to reinforce divisive tendencies among the local ruling families. Competition, rather than cooperation, became the norm among the elite.[17]

The Tagalog provinces had been the center of agitation for a greater Filipino participation in governing the Philippines during the last half of the 19th century. Laguna province, the birthplace of Jose Rizal, the leader of the reformist Propaganda Movement who was executed in 1896, was a center for nationalist and anti-Spanish activity. A series of revolts in the region began in 1872 failed, but discontent continued.[18] In 1896 the region responded to the *Katipunan* call-to-arms of Bonifacio and Aguinaldo. Miguel Malvar of Batangas and Juan Cailles of Laguna were among the elite who rallied to fight in support of the *Katipunan* cause. After the Spanish reconquered the provinces in 1897, local conditions became worse as "agricultural collapse led . . . to widespread malnutrition, and malnutrition, in turn contributed to the declining health of the populace."[19] On the return of Aguinaldo in 1898, the Tagalog provinces again rose in revolt and ousted the Spanish. Aguinaldo appointed Brigadier General Malvar as his commander in Batangas province, and later, Brigadier General Cailles as commander in Laguna and Tayabas provinces. As directed by Aguinaldo's government, they worked for over a year to build local military forces and militia. They linked those forces directly to the local elite in the towns who strongly supported the Tagalog cause. Sporadic fights in 1899 with the Americans along Laguna Bay occurred, but the primary focus remained the organization and defense of their provinces. Malvar, for example, made several defense plans for Batangas and defensive positions were prepared. However, the basic assumption for each plan was that the Americans would attack from the sea. When the Americans attacked from the north out of Cavite province in January 1900, Malvar's forces were in the wrong place. Their hasty attempts to contest the American advance failed, and in early February the *insurrectos* reorganized for guerrilla warfare.[20]

Tagalog *Insurrectos*

After the Americans overran southwestern Luzon, Trias directed his subordinates—Cailles in Laguna and Tayabas provinces and Malvar in Batangas province—to conduct guerrilla or ambush warfare. Trias had two outstanding guerrilla leaders. Both proved "capable, intelligent, and ruthless."[21] Cailles, son of a French father and Anglo-Indian mother, was born in Laguna province. A schoolteacher in Cavite province in 1896, he commanded a unit of the *Katipunan* during the revolt. On Aguinaldo's return in 1898, he served with the forces besieging Manila. Appointed brigadier general and governor of Laguna in 1899 at age 33, he had about a year to develop his local forces and their support system before the Americans arrived. Malvar, a successful landowner, businessman, and *principlia* from Santo Tomas in Batangas, had fought with Aguinaldo in 1896–97 and had accompanied him to Hong Kong. On return to the Philippines, Malvar became a brigadier general and the provincial commander for Batangas in 1898. Cailles and Malvar established firm control on the civil and military leaders in their provinces.[22]

Building on the support of the local Tagalog elite and the established militias in each town, Malvar and Cailles moved about their provinces in early 1900 establishing full-time guerrilla units raised and supported by each town. Malvar operated from a base in the mountains near the junction of where the three provinces came together to the west of Tiaong in Tayabas. Cailles operated in southern and eastern Laguna province. They selected officers with family, personal, or business ties to the local elite and often with similar ties to their provincial chief. They encouraged, supported, and reminded local civil leaders of their duties. In the fall,

Malvar clarified the organization and responsibilities in his proclamation "Guerrilla Warfare Instructions." In addition to its local militia, each town had a full-time guerrilla column armed with all the local firearms. The armed *insurrectos* were to hide and to harass the Americans by ambush and by disruption of their logistics and communications. The column was stationed in the town and surrounding barrios from which it drew recruits, food, supplies, and money. Local leaders worked directly with the guerrilla commander providing logistics, intelligence, and, at times, the local militia. Both the civil officials and military commanders were encouraged not to become a hindrance to one another. A typical column had 50 to 60 *insurrectos* and 20 to 30 firearms. Both Cailles and Malvar stressed firepower instead of numbers. Malvar limited the number of bolo men in his full-time units to no more than 30 percent. Weapons, limited in quantity and generally poorly maintained, restricted the size of the guerrilla units; but, a shortage of ammunition proved a bigger problem. Cailles, for example, had only 20 rounds per firearm at one time. With the American naval blockade in effect, the *insurrectos* were forced to manufacture their own ammunition, often of poor quality. However, even with these severe restrictions, the guerrillas were able to maintain control of the towns and to continue to harass American occupation forces.[23]

Initially all Tagalogs, not just the local leaders, were forbidden under penalty of death from any cooperation with the Americans. In fact, the Americans found many towns empty when they arrived. By the summer of 1900, pressure in American occupied towns caused this policy to change. Local leaders were permitted to work with the Americans as long as they continued their active support of the *insurrectos*. A system of parallel or shadow government evolved in which local leaders outwardly met the requirements of the American post commanders while continuing to support their local militia and guerrilla columns. In some places, guerrilla leaders met with local leaders to identify nominees to fill positions in the American local government. As a result, the leaders of the local American government were usually active civil or military leaders in the insurrection.[24] The support of the guerrillas and the militia—collecting taxes, providing food, gathering intelligence, and hiding *insurrectos* and weapons—continued undetected in American-occupied towns for over a year. Although inability to communicate and lack of cultural understanding compounded the American problem, the *insurrectos* in the Tagalog provinces found it "relatively easy . . . to mislead an army that was devoting so much of its attention to chasing the enemy's . . . [armed *insurrectos*] and so little to understanding the nature of the conflict."[25]

Unlike other places in the Philippines, the revolutionary infrastructure in the Tagalog provinces—resting on its dedicated local leadership—proved "the best organized and best led, and had the most popular support of any on the island."[26] When voluntary support wavered, coercion—varying in extremity from warnings to fines to arson to death—was common. *Insurrectos* attacked American supporters or *Americanistas* and their property. Both Malvar and Cailles encouraged the frequent and systematic use of coercion. Cailles deliberately publicized his actions as a warning to others. Although the exact number of assassinations is disputed, it was frequent enough to make the threat credible to the population.[27] Cailles instructions meant that:

> Indeed any native found rendering voluntary service to the Americans without contributing a large portion of his compensation to the insurrection, and any native who showed any friendship for Americans, or was suspected of being a spy for them, was, regardless of sex, marked for secret assassination by the insurgents or their emissaries. It was therefore not astonishing that the natives of this district with few exceptions rendered implicit obedience to the insurgent government.[28]

Even as late as the fall of 1901, an American officer wrote that the Tagalog *insurrectos* have the "aid of every inhabitant of the country for information, etc. They continue to dominate the inhabitants and compel their aid, active or passive, for the simple reason that their punishments for failure to comply are much more than any practiced by us, or permitted to us under the laws of civilized warfare."[29] Popular support for the insurrection, reinforced as necessary by coercion, sustained the Tagalog resistance in southwestern Luzon longer than anywhere else on Luzon.

Cailles and Malvar skillfully organized and guided guerrilla operations in their provinces. By attacking isolated American detachments, the *insurrectos* reinforced the American tendency to focus on the guerrillas. By avoiding battle, they frustrated the American desire for a quick, final end to the resistance. When guerrillas did strike, they struck quickly and then dispersed rapidly. An American officer complained:

> ... this country offers so many hiding places that the insurgents do not have to go far to obtain perfect concealment. And as a rule, after leaving the scene of combat they conceal their weapons and appear as innocent amigos. Most of them live at home and work at their ordinary vocation, those who are not at home live in houses already occupied by their friends and all appears to be one family in each

house. All this makes it almost impossible to find any particular band that had committed a certain depredation.[30]

At the same time, the *insurrectos* denied the Americans control of the population and of the countryside. Both Malvar and Cailles understood that the military activity of their militia and guerrilla forces was less important than their local political and psychological presence. As long as the militia existed, the Americans could not establish loyal civil government nor win the support of the population. An American commander noted, "I owe it to our rebel enemy to say that, from their standpoint, I regard their scheme of warfare as nearly perfect. In the facility with which they can play the *insurrecto–amigo* act, they have an immense advantage. Their facilities for recruitment and their plans for receiving money and supplies are not to be despised."[31] Isolated physically in small garrisons and living amongst a large, hostile, alien Tagalog population, the Americans were unaware of things hiding in plain sight. For example, an American report stated that Malvar:

> Goes about the country with an indian shirt and trousers cut off or rolled up to the knees and if captured will affect being a very simple, inoffensive and ignorant native who knows nothing and will give a wrong name. . . . He passed through American troops with a rooster under his arm, and has ridden a carabao through Santo Tomas and Lipa, stopping at Lipa to talk to the Presidente without being detected.[32]

Both Malvar and Cailles had close calls, but they were never captured. Each time they escaped it added to their mystique with their supporters. The same held true for the *insurrectos* living amongst the local populace. For the Americans in the Tagalog region, most *insurrectos*—guerrillas and civilian supporters—remained undetectable for over a year.

American Military Operations

The 1st Division oversaw the initial occupation of the Tagalog provinces. On 10 April 1900 the 1st Division was disestablished and replaced by the Department of Southern Luzon. The Department of Southern Luzon included an area of 10,000 square miles and a population of 1.2 million on southern Luzon and roughly the same size area with a smaller population on the islands of Marinduque, Masbate, Mindoro, and Samar. The department was divided into four districts—First through Fourth. Major General Bates,[33] a 60-year old Regular officer and the former commander of the 1st Division, commanded the Department of Southern Luzon. Having earned his rank by "the iron law of seniority," Bates proved to be a mediocre, methodical commander. He did not adjust to the guerrilla warfare in southern Luzon nor did he encourage his subordinates to do so.[34]

Second District, Department of Southern Luzon, consisted of the provinces of Batangas, Laguna, and Tayabas (see map 7). The former 1st Brigade commander, Brigadier General Wheaton, commanded Second District until 16 April when he departed to replace Major General Arthur MacArthur as commander of the Department of Northern Luzon. Colonel William E. Birkhimer, the intelligent, hard-charging commander of the 28th USV Infantry, served as the acting district commander until the arrival of 63-year old Brigadier General Robert H. Hall[35] who assumed command on 28 June. Sixteen months from retirement when he took command, Hall proved to be an indifferent commander in dealing with the *insurrectos*. Hall's apathy and Bates conservatism created a command climate in Second District not conducive to innovative pacification measures in the towns.[36] Destroying armed *insurrectos* dominated their attention.

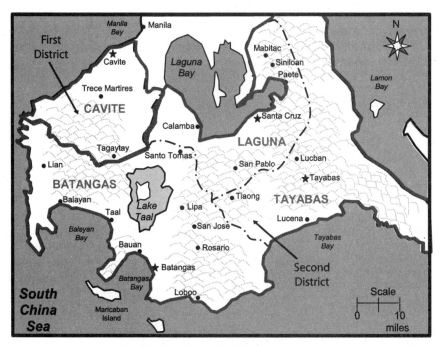

Map 7. Department of Southern Luzon.

With 5,000 of the 11,000 American troops in the Department of Southern Luzon, Second District was the most strongly garrisoned district. Even so, the troop strength was inadequate to garrison the towns and to establish control of the countryside. Colonel George S. Anderson, commanding the 38th USV Infantry, garrisoned southwestern Batangas

81

province. The 28th USV Infantry, commanded by Birkhimer, controlled southeastern Batangas province. Colonel Robert L. Bullard's 39th USV Infantry initially occupied four towns in north-central Batangas and eastern Laguna province. Colonel Cornelius Gardener's 30th USV Infantry controlled Tayabas province. One of two infantry regiments raised in the Philippines from state volunteer veterans in 1899, the 37th USV Infantry, commanded by Colonel Benjamin F. Cheatham, controlled northeast Laguna and parts of northern Tayabas.[37] Troops from the 6th Cavalry and the 11th USV Cavalry worked with the regimental commanders.

Although the population remained sullen and uncooperative, contact with armed *insurrectos* rarely occurred. In mid-February Wheaton had predicted that "although the predatory bands into which . . . the insurgent forces have degenerated are giving occasional trouble, these, I trust and believe, will be extirpated in short order. The pacification of the territory . . . will then be complete."[38] Destroying the armed *insurrectos* through aggressive operations would pacify the region and provide a secure environment for the establishment of local civil government and other pacification measures. In April Wheaton reminded his commanders:

> The importance of the greatest practicable activity in scouting the country and exterminating all hostile bands is urged. All concentration or organization of guerrilla bands will be prevented when it is known that such effort is being made. The greatest severity consistent with the laws of war is enjoined when armed parties of hostiles are encountered.[39]

In June Birkhimer stressed the importance of "killing armed insurrectos and ladrones and showing all people by our armed presence everywhere, that we are masters of the country and intend to remain so."[40] This reinforced the emphasis on military operations directed against the armed *insurrectos*. Local patrols and larger operations were constant; however, contact with the *insurrectos* was infrequent. From March to May only 11 engagements, most initiated by the *insurrectos*, took place in Second District with American casualties of one KIA and two WIA.[41] The *insurrectos* appeared weak and disorganized throughout the district.

Initial Operations

Although attempts to establish local governments in the spring of 1900 were hampered by basic flaws in General Orders 40 and 43, the principal obstacle remained the refusal of the local *principales* to work with the American post commanders. In fact, most of the population fled the towns when the Americans arrived. By March they were returning to their homes. Birkhimer maintained, "We must take care of the good and law abiding people who are now coming back and quieting down on their little farms all about, else we will lose that confidence in us that sound policy requires we should inspire and pursue."[42] The difficulty of doing this, given the support for the *insurrectos* in every town and the established *insurrecto* infrastructure, was not to be understood by Second District commanders for almost a year.

Part of the reason was the apparent ease with which Gardener reported pacification of Tayabas province. A staunch believer in pacification and in trusting the Tagalogs to work in good faith with the Americans, Gardener believed that "mere pills will be more effective than bullets." Within 6 months, Gardener established schools in each garrisoned town. In April he insisted that his post commanders establish a local government with a local police force. Reports of difficulties did not deter him. Major Matthew F. Steele, commander at Lucban, wrote he did "not expect a single person to vote" for the reason that "the edge of the bolo and the hand of an assassin are the price they would pay for taking that oath and holding office under American rule."[43] After repeated failures in Lucban, Gardener suggested that Steele do what he had done—lock the local leaders in a room until they established a government. When Steele tried this, the locals first elected an *insurrecto* leader in the local jail. Then they elected their three greatest opponents. The next time he tried, they fled and hid in a nearby town. Finally, Steele just appointed a local leader who then appealed directly to Bates who responded: "It is not the desire of the Department Commander that friendly natives should be placed in jeopardy by assuming office when we cannot assure their immunity from those who are still antagonistic; such offices should be assumed voluntarily."[44] After a frustrating 8-month effort, in December Steele wrote Gardener:

> I have tried every argument to persuade various citizens
> to accept the office of [*presidente*] . . . without success.
> They are all afraid of [assassination]. . . . Every principal
> man in Lucban has some property . . . [outside the town]
> and they all claim they would not be able to visit [it] . . .
> if they accepted the office. And they claim . . . that the
> insurgents would take away and destroy all their rice and
> other things . . . [outside the town]. They all say but for
> this they would gladly accept the office and they hope
> the conditions will soon be such that they can accept this
> office without risk to their lives and property.[45]

Despite this lack of security for local officials, Gardener reported the province peaceful. Incidents of lawlessness were attributed to local ladrones or to *insurrectos* from neighboring provinces, but never to *insurrectos* in Tayabas. Perhaps not surprisingly, Gardener reported Tayabas as ready for civil government in September.[46] The other Second District regimental commanders were not as optimistic as Gardener, did not share his trust of Tagalogs, and did not have the pacification successes Gardener reported. In fact, most would have agreed with a captain who wrote "This business of fighting and civilizing and educating at the same time doesn't mix very well. Peace is needed first."[47]

Peace did not come to southwestern Luzon in the summer of 1900. With the onset of the rainy season, Malvar and Cailles increased guerrilla attacks on isolated American detachments throughout each of the provinces. Cheatham reported that in Laguna province there was "renewed activity among the insurgents, taxes are being collected and soldiers impressed, the towns that are not occupied by the Americans and were full of men a month ago are now practically deserted except for women and children." In southeastern Batangas, Birkhimer added, "we control within the lines of our bayonets, but no further." Between June and August engagements increased by over 400 percent from the preceding 3 months. Despite higher *insurrecto* losses, the 54 actions inflicted losses of 12 KIA and 28 WIA on the Americans.[48]

The increased tempo of operations could not have come at a worse time for the Americans. Worn by constant patrolling and incessant military operations and with the onset of the rainy season, sick rates climbed: 25 percent for the 37th USV Infantry in Laguna province and 30 percent for both the 30th USV Infantry in Tayabas province and for the 39th USV Infantry in central Batangas. Some garrisons were particularly unhealthy. At one time, the post at Paete in Laguna province had only 30 soldiers fit for duty out of 101 assigned. At Tiaong in northwest Tayabas province, an infantry company had less than 10 men fit for duty, which meant many of the sick remained on duty.[49] Disease alone created half-strength companies. Out of an assigned strength of 49 officers and 1,230 soldiers, the 39th USV Infantry had 24 officers and 720 soldiers fit for duty that summer. During its tour in the Philippines, the 39th USV Infantry had 13 KIA and 30 WIA and 111 deaths from disease.[50] Throughout the Philippines in 1900, three times as many soldiers died from disease than were killed or died of wounds. In fact, dysentery alone killed as many soldiers as the total wounded. From January through July, out of 995 American deaths, 654 died from disease. Almost twice as many soldiers, 1,560, were shipped to the United States: 1,147 for medical treatment, 303 for disability discharges, and 110 as insane.[51] Inadequate medical care and a shortage of medicine meant that the sick tended to stay sick or got worse while the healthy—overworked and lacking rest from troop shortages and increased *insurrecto* activity—became ill. At the beginning of July, Hall assumed command of Second District from Birkhimer. Faced with a declining troop strength and increased *insurrecto* activity, he changed the policy of constant military activity to one of responding to known *insurrecto* threats. Soldiers would remain in garrison, performing local security and pacification duties, until they had intelligence about an *insurrecto* activity or location. Then they would react.[52]

The frustration of combating guerrilla warfare, of operating in a hostile alien population, and of conducting innumerable operations—for example, a hike of 120 miles in 7 days—in pursuit of a phantom foe that struck when and where it desired took its toll. Many American soldiers—predisposed by the attitudes of the time to view Filipinos as inferior—"came in time to view them as savages and to hate them—combatants and noncombatants alike."[53] Anderson in southeastern Batangas wrote, "They are rank barbarians, not much above our better class of indians."[54] At times, both Americans and *insurrectos* resorted to harsh, even illegal, actions. Despite repeated prohibitions, unofficial American interrogation techniques included the water cure and the rope cure. At the same time, official military measures became harsher—sometimes intentionally and sometimes inadvertently. In July, commenting on sweeps to round up Tagalog suspects, Birkhimer noted:

> . . . we do not know insurrectos and bad men from good ones, so we are often compelled to arrest all alike and bring them in here to be sorted out; in this way the good are temporarily inconvenienced, but only temporarily. But even this evil has a good side: the people find that the United States authorities are liable to overhaul them at any moment and it has a salutary, lasting effect.[55]

Few Tagalogs shared his assessment. Once the distinction between potential friend and definite enemy no longer mattered, indiscriminate arrests led to other indiscriminate actions like the destruction of property. In the summer of 1900 it became common in the Tagalog provinces for Americans to burn houses that *insurrectos* had fired from, that were used to store supplies for the *insurrectos*, and that happened to be near destroyed telegraph lines. Although initially Gardener and Birkhimer protested these actions as counterproductive, they became common. Cheatham encouraged his troops searching for Cailles "to burn freely and kill every man who runs."[56] Anderson recommended "a thorough destruction of all stores that may serve as subsistence to the Insurgent Army."[57]

The Americans did have some successes. An informer warned the post commander at Taal in Batangas province of an imminent *insurrecto* attack. The post commander took no precautions, and Malvar and 400 *insurrectos* attacked a small garrison on 16 July. Six Americans were wounded. Birkhimer reacted promptly and cornered part of the *insurrectos* the next day. On one of those rare opportunities where an *insurrecto* force stayed and fought, the Americans were able to attack with the support of the river gunboat *Villalobos* and killed 38 *insurrectos*. An officer hailed Birkhimer as "the champion *insurrecto* exterminator in the islands."[58] Hall even recommended him for a brevet to brigadier general. Cheatham had one success against Cailles after searching most of the summer. On 5 August a detachment from the 37th USV Infantry and 11th USV Cavalry, led by a native guide, discovered Cailles' camp. In the ensuing fight, five *insurrectos* were killed and eight rifles captured. More importantly, the Americans captured the papers and correspondence of Cailles.[59]

Despite these successes by the Americans in southern Luzon, things did not improve during the summer. Bates summarized the situation on 15 August in his annual report:

> I cannot recommend the reduction of the forces in this command by so much as a single soldier. . . . A single battalion can today march from one end of this department to the other without encountering enough resistance from the enemy to impede seriously its progress, but small parties of troops cannot leave the garrisoned posts without incurring a danger of attack. . . . The insurrectos, after making an attack, disperse, assume civilian garb, and conceal themselves among the peaceful inhabitations, often taking up their residence and continuing their conspiracy in towns occupied by our troops, where they terrorize the mass of inhabitants by threatening condign punishment to those who display friendship toward Americans. When captured and again set free, they have shown their lack of appreciation of the policy of magnanimity by again appearing in arms against us at the first opportunity. The necessity of ferreting out, running down, and punishing this hostile minority . . . and our moral obligation to protect our friends render it necessary to have troops stationed at all places where civil government is established; for the absence of troops means the presence of anarchy. It will doubtless be a long time before any diminution can be made in all of the garrisons of this department.[60]

Pacification was not working. Lack of security was considered the problem. Destroying the armed *insurrectos*, not the support infrastructure, remained the solution.

Following Aguinaldo's instructions, Malvar and Cailles supplemented their routine sniping and harassment of American forces by increased attacks during the fall of 1900 with 10 attacks in September and 11 in October.[61] A couple of battles were fought on terms favorable to the *insurrectos*. On 17 September an American officer with just 2 days in the Philippines attacked a large force of *insurrectos* entrenched at Mabitac in Laguna province. What followed was the worst American defeat on Luzon during the insurrection. MacArthur reported to the War Department:

> Capt. David D. Mitchell, Fifteenth Infantry, 90 men, Company L, Fifteenth Infantry, from Siniloan, Laguna Province, attacked insurgent General Cailles, who had 800 men in position at Mavitac, same province. Desperate fight ensued, which was pushed from the front with great pertinacity by Mitchell across causeway and through water waist deep; cooperative attack under Capt. Georg F. Cooke, Fifteenth Infantry, with 40 men, Company K, Fifteenth Infantry, and 10 men, Company B, Thirty-seventh Infantry, US Volunteers; could not reach enemy's position because of high water in arm of lake, which could not be crossed; entire country was afloat in consequence rains; this very much impeded offensive action. After hour twenty minutes' fighting command withdrew to Siniloan. . . . [next day] insurgents had escaped . . . most of them no doubt going back into contiguous barrios to appear for time being, or until called into fight again, as peaceful amigos. . . . [American force of 4 officers and 130 soldiers lost 2 officers and 22 men KIA and 1 officer and 18 men WIA]. . . . Thirty-three per cent is profoundly impressive loss and indicates stubbornness of fight, fearless leadership of officers and splendid response of men. Insurgent loss, as far as known, 10 killed, 20 wounded.[62]

Despite the praise for his officers and men in his telegram, MacArthur told Commissioner William H. Taft that Mitchell would have faced court-martial if he had lived. The next day, Cailles returned the bodies of eight Americans with all their personal effects.[63] Another sustained fight occurred in northwest Batangas province where over 400 *insurrectos* attacked a 21-man American detachment on 21 October. During a 4-hour fight in which the *insurrectos* held the high ground, many *insurrectos* fired black-powder weapons that offset their tactical advantage and permitted the Americans to locate their positions. The Americans lost 2 KIA and 4 WIA to an estimated 100 *insurrecto* casualties.[64] In mid-October Bates expressed a concern with American reports of enemy actions throughout his department. He directed, "The use of the word 'Ambushed' or 'Ambuscade' is wrong, in that it indicates lack of precaution on the part of our officers and men, which is not the case. The use of these words is therefore liable to misapprehension and criticism, and should be avoided." He suggested that "attacked" was the appropriate term unless the soldiers were actually surprised by a lack of proper precautions.[65] Predictably, *insurrecto* ambushes decreased, but their attacks increased.

Throughout the fall, American operations against the guerrillas forced some bands away from the towns, but they did not reduce *insurrecto* support from nor grip on the population. On 27 October Malvar issued a proclamation providing detailed instructions to both his guerrilla leaders and to the local leaders on their duties and responsibilities to one another in resisting the American occupation.[66] Cailles instructed his commanders on 15 November that:

> The foundation of your methods will be to protect our friends and punish traitors of all kinds. If any citizen accepts office from the enemy, that will cause his condemnation to death, the destruction of his house and the confiscation of his property, which will be delivered to the treasury for the support of the revolution. If on account of any obstacle, you are not able to carry out these orders, or if any of the people protect the traitor, thus showing respect for his illegitimate authority, you will destroy their houses without hesitation or delay, and you will take no care to stop the spread of the fire. You will be responsible to me alone, and then only for lack of zeal in obeying me.[67]

Before December, to include MacArthur's June to September amnesty offer, only 30 *insurrectos* had surrendered in the entire Department of Southern Luzon.[68] This strong indication of the solidarity of the Tagalog population and the dedication of the guerrillas meant that pacification—the destruction of the guerrillas and the support of the population—had failed in southern Luzon.

MacArthur's Campaign Measures

Although the re-election of McKinley had little effect on the *insurrectos* in the Department of Southern Luzon, MacArthur's new campaign that began in late December to separate the guerrillas from their support in the towns had an effect throughout the Philippines in 1901. The declaration of martial law under General Orders 100 (see appendix B), the proclamation to the Filipino populace explaining its obligations as noncombatants under military law and the American intent to strictly enforce military law (see appendix C), the establishment of provost courts to try civilian supporters of the guerrillas, the establishment of a local police, the increase of Filipino auxiliaries, the imprisonment of POWs for the duration of the insurrection, and the establishment of the pro-American Federal Party seriously challenged the *insurrectos* in southern Luzon where American troop levels remained constant at the beginning of 1901 as Regulars—1st and 6th Cavalry and 4th, 8th, 21st, and 30th Infantry—began replacing the USV regiments that had been in place for over a year.[69]

Bates and Hall had resisted arming Tagalogs from the beginning of their commands. Despite MacArthur's directives and successes elsewhere, their resistance continued. Little was accomplished in Second District, beyond the actions of a few post commanders, in creating a local police force until mid-1901 when the provinces shifted from military to civilian control.[70] Bates and Hall continued to resist the recruitment of native auxiliaries. Concerns of loyalty and a scarcity of potential recruits meant that neither scout units nor other irregular forces, common in other parts of the Philippines, were used in Second District. In fact, Tagalog units recruited from outside the district were not used until June 1901.[71] No action had been taken on Birkhimer's summer of 1900 recommendation to form a district intelligence section to collect, analyze, and distribute information. As a result, intelligence collection and sharing within the department and district remained sporadic and fragmented.[72] However, the Division of Military Information in Manila, created in December by MacArthur, provided in February 1901 all post commanders a comprehensive list of 560 guerrilla leaders in the Tagalog provinces identified from the 22 December 1900 capture of the papers of Trias in Cavite province.[73] The department and district commanders provided no guidance or program for local commanders in pursuing MacArthur's goal of separating the guerrillas from their infrastructure in the towns. Garrison commanders continued to struggle with the problems of local civil government in towns controlled by the *insurrecto* infrastructure.

The Federal Party pursued the surrender of *insurrecto* leaders through discussions and appeals beginning in February 1901. Responding to this serious threat on 28 February, Cailles directed that all *federalistas* and others seeking peace should be immediately shot without trial:

> When any agent of the Federal Party or any of its adherents can not be captured through being constantly with the enemy, or guarded by him the heads of the pueblos and the commander of columns will procure the execution of this agent even within the American lines by using for the purpose persons of known decision and of patriotism worthy of all praise.[74]

The first and biggest success of the Federal Party came when Trias, the commander for southern Luzon, surrendered after negotiations with the *federalistas*. Two weeks later, Trias addressed an appeal to his former *insurrecto* leaders in southern Luzon to surrender.[75] MacArthur reported to Washington:

> Mariano Trias, only lieutenant-general insurgent army, surrendered March 15 . . . with 9 officers, 199 well-armed men. Trias immediately took oath of allegiance presence several thousand natives; most auspicious event indicates final stage armed insurrection. Prestige Trias Southern Luzon equal that Aguinaldo.[76]

The *insurrecto* cause suffered a greater setback days afterward with the capture of Aguinaldo by the Americans. In April, Aguinaldo made a similar appeal for his followers to accept American government.

Reorganization and New Commanders

Malvar and Cailles responded to the decapitation of the *insurrecto* cause by meeting with guerrilla leaders in early April. On reconfirming their determination to continue their resistance and never to surrender, Malvar issued a proclamation on 12 April addressed to his "Brothers and Companions in the Strife" that announced, in accordance with a June 1900 decree, that he was replacing Trias as leader of the insurrection in southern Luzon. He appealed for the support of all Tagalogs, not just the local elite. On 28 April, Malvar issued 20 regulations that thoroughly reorganized the *insurrecto* movement in southern Luzon. Designed to improve guerrilla operations, to encourage resupply and recruitment, and to eliminate conflict between civilians and the guerrillas, these comprehensive regulations included reorganization of the guerrilla bands with an emphasis on ambush and protracted war, creation of a reserve supported by a draft of 1 man for every 100 men, imposition of a head tax on every person, and commissioning of any man able to raise and lead a guerrilla unit. Early in 1901 Malvar had divided Batangas province into three zones. Cailles now established local commanders for Laguna and Tayabas provinces. They both worked to strengthen the *insurrectos* in Tayabas where the guerrillas, nominally commanded by Colonel Eustacio Maloles, Malvar's brother-in-law, were fragmented, disorganized, and ineffective. The *insurrecto* civil infrastructure in Tayabas proved stronger than its guerrilla organization.[77] From February 1900 to January 1901, there were only 19 engagements in Tayabas province.[78] Despite the setbacks of March and April, the *insurrectos* in the Tagalog provinces appeared determined and were reorganizing to continue the struggle indefinitely.

The American departmental and district commanders changed at about this same time. Hall, the district commander, had requested relief in March. On 10 April the First District—basically Cavite province—and the Second District were reorganized as the First District, Department of Southern Luzon (see map 7). Brigadier General Samuel S. Sumner,[79] the 59-year old district commander in Cavite where Trias's surrender had practically ended resistance, assumed command of the combined district. A month later, Brigadier General James F. Wade, an old cavalryman, replaced Bates as commander of the Department of Southern Luzon. Although Wade may have understood the problem of guerrilla war in the Philippines somewhat better than Bates, he operated in the same mode as Bates.[80] Although the Wade-Sumner team would continue the uninspired, ineffectual civil governmental policies of their predecessors, Sumner proved to be more astute and involved in counterguerrilla operations than Hall had been.[81]

Sumner ordered 1,000 soldiers from Cavite as reinforcements for an offensive against Cailles and Malvar that began 23 May and continued until 1 July. He hoped that, as in Cavite province, a concentrated military effort would force them to surrender.[82] In mid-April Cailles had sworn never to surrender "while life lasts." On 26 April Cailles narrowly escaped death or capture, but in the process lost his personal effects, correspondence, and most of his staff. His entire infrastructure in Laguna province was compromised. Cailles suspended operations and asked for a meeting to negotiate with the Americans and the *federalistas*. Wade told Sumner to inform Cailles "that operations will not be suspended for one moment, that the time for conferences has gone by, and that no propositions from General Cailles will be entertained except unconditional surrender."[83] Rebuffed, Cailles intensified his efforts against the Americans. In May a *federalista* agent from Trias to Cailles received the same request for suspension of operations and negotiations. Sumner again refused. At the end of May, Wade reported:

Captain Davis struck the trail of Cailles. . . . He is said to have forty cavalry and fifty infantry, fully equipped. Cailles is very sick, and is being carried in a hammock. This information, obtained from captured soldier of the enemy, was confirmed by the inhabitants of house where he stops and by the natives along his trail. Cailles's force is scattered completely in the mountains, and all trace of him is lost.[84]

However, the tempo of operations had its effect. On 24 June Cailles surrendered in Laguna province. MacArthur reported to Washington: "General Cailles surrendered to-day Santa Cruz, Luzon, 386 rifles, 4,000 rounds ammunition, about 600 officers, men; has taken oath of allegiance; very important, as it is most probable pacification all southern Luzon will follow quickly."[85] Cailles, the ultimate "I-will-never-be-taken-alive" *insurrecto* leader, received $5,000 in gold for his weapons. In a short time, he would be appointed civil governor of Laguna province and become a ruthlessly effective *Americanista* in hunting down his former comrades.[86] Nevertheless, MacArthur's hope for the quick pacification of southern Luzon proved false. On 13 July, in open letters to Aguinaldo and Trias, Malvar declared himself commander of all *insurrectos* and urged all Filipinos to oppose the Americans.[87]

Sumner's military operations against Malvar yielded a different result in Batangas province. His sweeps produced minimal results. On 10 June *insurrectos* near Lipa overwhelmed a detachment of the 21st Infantry, killing two officers, one soldier, and one Filipino scout and wounding two soldiers. This reverse startled Sumner. A week later Sumner reported:

> The operations of this command have demonstrated that a well organized force of considerable strength control this country and are paid and subsisted by the inhabitants. General Malvar exercises supreme command. . . . While we have found several of his camps and destroyed them, it has been impossible to overtake this force or damage it to any extent. It has been found almost impossible to gain any information owing to fear or sympathy of natives. . . . They pay a regular tax and every barrio is a supply depot for the insurrectos whose homes and relatives are in their midst.[88]

He requested reinforcements and recommended harsher measures against noncombatants. Specifically Sumner advocated the arrest of all men, requiring them to surrender weapons and to provide information about the *insurrectos*. Failure to comply would mean imprisonment for the duration of the insurrection and the exile of local leaders outside the Philippines. He further advocated the burning and destruction of property to "bring a speedy end to the present unsettled and dangerous condition of affairs" in Batangas.[89] Wade responded by providing the reinforcements, but they were delayed until mid-July and included all the infantry requested but none of the cavalry. The recommendations for dealing with the populace were not approved. Wade's constraints restricted Sumner's effectiveness in pressuring the guerrilla bands and in cutting off their support from the populace. On 2 August Sumner submitted a bleak assessment. It was impossible to get reliable information, useless to pursue guerrillas who refuse to fight, and dangerous to move detachments. Malvar remained in control of the province. Sumner added his soldiers were "paralyzed for want of accurate information. They wander about the country, to the great detriment of their health, without any adequate result to find perhaps on their return that they were on the opposite of the hill, or quietly looking at them from some barrio."[90] Admitting that "the amount of country actually controlled by us is about as much as can be covered by the fire from our guns," Sumner recommended the creation of a bureau of information, the destruction of all barrios used by the *insurrectos*, the destruction of all supplies in the countryside, the closing of all ports in Batangas and Laguna provinces, and the deportation to Guam of supporters of the *insurrectos*. Wade acted on none of his recommendations.[91]

What Sumner and Wade did not realize was that their operations had made life harder for the guerrilla bands that were pushed further into the countryside. Malvar had appointed Lieutenant Colonel Pedro Caballes to command guerrillas in Laguna province. By September Caballes had 12 detachments with 750 rifles.[92] Later that fall he reported to Malvar:

> General, I cannot regulate the towns in my jurisdiction, because the traitor Cailles is always hunting for me with a force of American soldiers. . . . there are one hundred towns which do not want more war, and will tranquilly recognize the supreme authority of the United States. For the rest, the traitor Cailles, who is trying to catch me, is putting municipal officers in the towns of this province in order to establish a civil government.[93]

In Laguna province, which had been placed under civilian control in July, Cailles worked for the Americans to break the linkage between the towns and the guerrillas. In Batangas province, under military control after 17 July, Wade had not supported Sumner's measures to pressure the populace and local leaders. Relying on the assessments of local commanders and lacking an independent information section at district or department, Wade and Sumner had little understanding of the decline in guerrilla and civilian morale that American patrolling and operations caused.[94]

Sumner correctly assessed that Malvar could not mass forces for any length of time, nor would he. Malvar's policy was described by Sumner as "one of negative opposition as far as our Government is concerned, and a reign of terror as far as the natives."[95] On 4 September Sumner wrote Wade that "what the troops need is accurate information, if this could be obtained their work would be effective, and an end would be put to this irritating and troublesome rebellion in a short time."[96] After no response from Wade on his recommendation for a properly staffed and resourced district bureau of information, Sumner reported on 28 September the establishment in his district of "a system of general information between posts and these Headquarters as will enable Post Commanders to act promptly and intelligently on receipt of news."[97] That same day, Major General Adna R. Chaffee, commander of the Division of the Philippines and subordinate of Governor Taft since 4 July, issued General Orders 294 that required all post and field commanders to appoint an intelligence officer and to submit all military information through their commands to the Division of Military Information in Manila where the data would be collated, analyzed, and developed into information for units being assigned to areas with which they have no previous experience.[98]

Things would change dramatically in the Philippines in September and October. Chaffee reported to the War Department on 2 September:

> The disturbance in Wade's Department has contracted practically to Batangas Province, but here no serious impression has been made on Malvar's party, generally supposed to be from five hundred to six hundred strong scattered in the mountains and brush. Small parties have been struck, some surrenders made, but nothing done yet to press Malvar hard enough to get a squeal out of him, except that he asserts as do others who know him, that have come in, that he will never surrender. Campaigning there now is very difficult and while I have urged Wade and Sumner to be active and to give Malvar no rest, it results mainly in filling our hospitals with sick men, principally bowel cases.[99]

On 28 September Sumner wrote, "There are few means at hand to impress these people with the disadvantage of warfare unless we burn the barrios, destroy the food, and subject them to personal torture which is inhuman and unwise."[100] Appearing to reverse his call for harsher methods, Sumner's timing could not have been worse. On that day, an *insurrecto* attack destroyed all but 4 of the 74-man American garrison at Balangiga on the island of Samar—44 killed, 22 wounded, and 4 missing. This "massacre" served as a call for the prompt destruction of the insurrection on Samar and in Batangas province.[101]

Chaffee, a cavalryman who had risen from the ranks during the American Civil War, had little regard for civilians in general and for Governor Taft in particular. In early October, President Theodore Roosevelt cabled Chaffee: "I am deeply chagrined, to use the mildest possible term, over the trouble between yourself and Taft. I wish you to see him personally and to spare no effort to secure prompt and friendly agreements in regard to the differences between you."[102] For his part, Taft regularly wrote to the Secretary of War Elihu Root expressing his views of Chaffee, just as he had expressed his views of Governor-General MacArthur. On 14 October Taft wrote Root that Chaffee was not committed to pacification and that Chaffee believed the only way to achieve peace was to pin down the Filipinos "with bayonets for ten years until they submit."[103] Taft further opined, "General Wade is incompetent and General Sumner who is under him is not very much better."[104] Despite their disagreements, Taft and Chaffee agreed that the insurrection on Samar and in Batangas had to be destroyed, that it required harsh measures, and that new commanders were needed. In early November, Taft approved a law that made it illegal to advocate Philippine independence.[105] As requested by Chaffee on 9 November, the War Department reorganized the Division of the Philippines into two departments. Major General Wheaton commanded the Department of North Philippines which included Luzon and Wade departed to command the Department of South Philippines.[106] The Department of North Philippines was divided into seven separate brigades—First through Seventh. The Third Separate Brigade encompassed Batangas, Laguna, western Tayabas, and the island of Mindoro[107] (see map 8).

Third Separate Brigade Pacification of Southwestern Luzon, December 1901–April 1902

Chaffee began preparations for the campaign in southern Luzon. In Manila he met with members of the Federal Party on 12 November. Committees were appointed to approach Malvar and his commanders seeking surrender. A deadline of 31 December was placed on these efforts to negotiate.[108] A week later, Chaffee selected Brigadier General J. Franklin Bell,[109] the experienced and capable commander of the First District of the

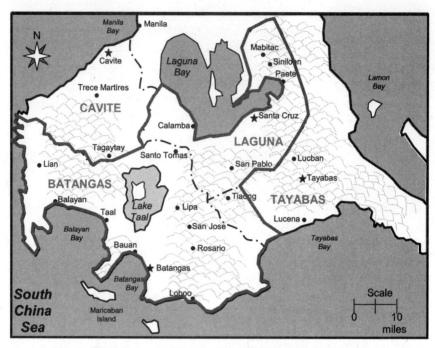

Map 8. Third Separate Brigade, Department of North Philippines.

Department of Northern Luzon, to command the Third Separate Brigade. Sumner departed to command the First Separate Brigade. As of 1 December the Division of the Philippines had 37,349 American soldiers assigned, down from 48,000 in July.[110] To increase native troops, in September Chaffee had established the Philippine Scouts from existing native scout units. The Philippine Scouts were recruited for 3 years, organized into 104-man companies, and commanded by an American lieutenant. Over 3,000 strong when created, the Scouts consisted of 34 companies—13 Ilocano, 11 Macabebe, 4 Tagalog, 4 Cagayan, and 2 Bicol. Six companies had been assigned to southern Luzon.[111] Chaffee assigned the Third Separate Brigade 7,600 American soldiers—1st and 6th Cavalry; 8th, 20th, 21st, 28th, and 30th Infantry; and 680 Philippine Scouts—companies of Macabebes, Ilocanos, and Tagalogs.[112]

After taking 2 weeks to assess the situation, Bell assumed command of the Third Separate Brigade on 30 November. Building on his experience as regimental commander in central Luzon, provost marshal in Manila, and district commander in the Ilocos, Bell developed a campaign plan that addressed the specific situation in his new area of operations. In a lengthy meeting on 1 December, Bell explained to the officers of the brigade

96

assembled in the town of Batangas what he intended to do and why. Bell said, "We have only one purpose, and that is to force the insurgents and those in active sympathy with them to want peace. In accomplishing this we must pay particular attention to the attitude of *principales* who live in the towns under our protection and are the eyes and ears and business agents of insurgents outside." Bell emphasized, "we must make the *principales* the object of our especial study and effort." He added, "We owe the Pacific people protection and must adopt some way of demonstrating our ability to give it. We must then show our intention to punish insurgents and those who aid and assist them." He explained that leniency had not worked, that "all the people of Batangas can have peace whenever they want it, and it should be our mission to make them want it as soon as we can by legitimate methods." Bell later distributed copies of General Orders 100 (appendix A) to each post commander stating, "we shall hereafter conduct war in accordance with that order." Although drastic measures would be required, Bell explained it was not necessary that they be implemented in a harsh, humiliating, or overbearing manner. In dealing with the populace, Bell wanted his soldiers to be "considerate and courteous in manner, but firm and relentless in action" while letting "acts, not words, convey your meaning." He summarized, "By cruel outrages and inhuman expedients, insurgents have created a reign of terror . . . which intimidates the people against giving any assistance, but by legitimate means we must produce sufficient fear of *our* power to at least prevent their helping insurgents." Bell continued, "It is my purpose, by giving them proper protection, to turn the inhabitants against the insurrection and secure their earnest and loyal assistance in efforts to re-establish peace." Bell ended the meeting, "As soon as I have studied the situation a few days, I shall begin the issuance of definite written instructions."[113]

Although military operations continued during December, Bell focused his attention on setting the conditions for a counterguerrilla effort that would begin 1 January 1902. On 3 December he established a brigade intelligence officer and appointed six officers with Ilocos experience— three from the 3d Cavalry and three from the 20th Infantry—to conduct provost courts. Their task was to investigate the *insurrecto* infrastructure in the towns, to gather intelligence, and to prosecute those who supported the guerrillas.[114] Two days later detailed instructions for provost courts and information collection were provided to all post commanders.[115] At the end of December, a brigade prison had been established at the town of Batangas.[116]

At the same time, Bell provided his policies with detailed guidance to his post commanders in a series of telegraphic circulars. Of the 38 circulars issued during the campaign, the 22 issued in December set the conditions and focus of the campaign that ensued. On 8 December post commanders were ordered to establish a zone of protection within the physical limits of each town to house the population from the country-side that had until 25 December to move there with all their property and foodstuffs. After 25 December all persons outside the zones of protection were to be considered hostile and all properties outside the zones of protection liable to confiscation or destruction. Bell's stated purpose was to "put an end to enforced contributions, now levied by insurgents . . . by means of intimidation and assassination" and to "furnish protection to inhabitants . . . against the depredations of armed insurgents." On the establishment of peace, the populace would be encouraged and assisted in returning to their homes.[117] The next day, Bell explained in detail his policy "that will as soon as possible make the people want peace and want it badly." Emphasizing provisions from General Orders 100, Bell addressed his expectations of local leaders and the actions to be taken if they were not met.

> The only acceptable and convincing evidence of the real sentiments of either individuals or town councils should be such acts publicly performed as must inevitably commit them irrevocably to the side of the Americans by arousing the animosity and opposition of the insurgent element. Such acts are reliable evidence, but mere words are worthless. . . . Neutrality should not be tolerated. Every inhabitant of this Brigade should either be an active friend or be classed as an enemy.[118]

Provost courts dealt with disloyal inhabitants. Police no longer received pay without demonstrated public support for the Americans. On 13 December Bell stressed that the illegal status of guerrillas, their active supporters, and their "flagrant violations of the laws of war" left him no option but the enforcement of the strictest punishments permitted under General Orders 100. Bell threatened to execute *insurrecto* POWs if Americans or their supporters were assassinated.[119] Assassinations ceased at once. Along with the circulars addressing keeping food out of the hands of *insurrectos*, Bell established his basic plan for dealing with the infrastructure—concentrating the population into zones of protection secured by American forces, pressuring local leaders to take actions in support of the Americans, and controlling food supplies.

Continuing to emphasize the provisions of General Orders 100, Bell further tightened his hold on the population at the end of December. Post commanders were directed to sweep the areas around their towns from 26 to 31 December to collect all foodstuffs for feeding the inhabitants of their zones of protection, if necessary.[120] On 21 December all traffic outside the towns was forbidden effective 1 January 1902.[121] Two days later, the arrest of local leaders not actively supporting the Americans was directed as a means to prosecute the guilty and to intimidate the neutral.[122] The activities of the population were further restricted on 24 December when a curfew was established and activities curtailed—for example, cockfighting was forbidden and markets suspected of collecting funds for the *insurrectos* closed.[123] That same day, local Tagalog leaders received additional duties for reporting *insurrecto* activity and supporting the Americans. Failure meant appearance before a provost court.[124] Bell reminded his commanders on 24 December that the "primary and most important object of all our operations in this brigade is to obtain possession of the arms now in the hands of insurgents and disloyal persons, and incidentally to capture as many insurgents as possible."[125] Surrendered firearms—each worth a 30-peso reward—increased at the end of December. Bell proscribed bolos on 28 December.[126] At the end of December, Bell summarized the activities of December for his post commanders:

> The purpose of the preceding telegraphic circulars of instruction has been to place the burden of the war on the disloyal and to so discipline them that they will become anxious to aid and assist the government in putting an end to the insurrection and in securing the re-establishment of civil government. Their provisions are based upon the assumption that, with very few exceptions, practically the whole population has been hostile to us at heart. In order to combat such a population, it is necessary to make the state of war insupportable, and there is no more efficacious way of accomplishing this than by keeping the minds of the people in such a state of anxiety and apprehension that living under such conditions will become unbearable.[127]

With the population concentrated and controlled, the local leadership torn between loyalty to the guerrillas and intense, personal pressure from the Americans, and the constant efforts by post commanders and provost courts to ferret out the local infrastructure, the Americans began to receive information, support, and weapons in some towns.

On 27 December Bell provided Wheaton an assessment of his upcoming operation. Convinced that within 2 months no insurrection would exist in his area of operations, Bell expressed that his "only fear" was that the *insurrectos* would bury their weapons and scatter. His control of the population and the towns would not permit them to remain in his area of operations. Bell planned to take about half of his troops, divide them into columns of 50 men each, and sweep areas of known *insurrecto* activity. He acknowledged:

> . . . no such strength is necessary to cope with all the insurgents in the Philippine Islands, but the country is indescribably rough and badly cut up, the ravines and mountains. I take so large a command for the purpose of thoroughly searching each ravine, valley, and mountain peak for insurgents and for food, expecting to destroy everything I find outside of towns, all able-bodied men will be killed or captured. Old men, women and children will be sent to towns. This movement begins January 1, by which time I hope to have nearly all the food supply in the towns.[128]

Beginning with the Loboo Mountains in southeast Batangas, Bell planned next to move to Lake Taal to clear western Batangas, and then to concentrate his forces east of Lipa. That would be followed by operations into the mountains north of Lipa along the tri-province border where Malvar normally operated and finally by a move into the mountains along the southern Batangas–Tayabas boundary. Bell planned to accompany his troops during these operations. With the population concentrated and travel restricted, Bell was confident the *insurrectos* would be on the run and could not stand the strain and lack of food for more than 2 months. Not optimistic about the on-going efforts of the Federal Party negotiators, Bell reminded Wheaton that their passes expired on 31 December.[129]

Beginning on 1 January 1902, initial operations in the Loboo Mountains by two columns of 1,800 Americans yielded little contact and killed only 9 *insurrectos*, but caused significant destruction of supplies in just a week. Besides burning over 6,000 structures, the Americans captured or destroyed over 1,400 tons of rice, hundreds of bushels of corn, hundreds of hogs and chickens, and over 200 carabaos, 800 cattle, and 680 horses.[130] Bell then sent them back into the Loboo Mountains with instructions that their "common object [was] the complete clearing out of every vestige of animal life and every particle of food supply found within the region."[131] After 10 January Bell reported that the Americans faced "no armed encounter worthy of record."[132] In one area after another, the insurgents were kept constantly on the move. On 13 January Colonel Anastacio Marasigan surrendered at Taal with 21 officers, 245 *insurrectos*, and 219 rifles.[133] The cumulative effect of these sweeps was the end of guerrilla activity near Lake Taal in early January and near the town of Batangas in late January. In early February the *insurrecto* battalion in Lipa surrendered and the key leaders were cooperative with the Americans by the end of the month.[134] Even Cailles organized volunteers from Laguna province to accompany American units into the mountains.[135] Cut off from the population and fleeing widespread American operations, *insurrectos* began surrendering individually and in small units. Military operations continued to sweep areas of known guerrilla activity through March and into April.

Work among the towns continued in concert with military operations. The majority of Bell's eight telegraphic circulars in January focused on ensuring adequate food for the zones of protection and on preventing food from falling into the hands of the *insurrectos*. To prevent an outbreak of small pox, Bell instituted an immunization program in the zones of protection.[136] Bell recalled veterans from the Ilocos region to help destroy the infrastructure in the towns. Crispulo Patajo, Bell's former chief of detectives in the First District of the Department of Northern Luzon, served in Batangas as his chief of scouts. William T. Johnston, promoted to captain, was assigned provost court duty and sent to Lipa, which Bell called "the worst town in the brigade." Within 2 weeks, Johnston cleaned out the *insurrecto* infrastructure there. His investigation revealed "that all the influential people . . . had been all the time actively engaged in assisting and prolonging the insurrection." He arrested 172 tax collectors and agreed to release one for every two rifles surrendered. Those not released were imprisoned for the duration. A local volunteer unit was formed to act as guides for the Americans. Johnston forced the *principales* to sign a letter renouncing their past actions and promising support for Americans. He then sent that letter to Manila where it was publicized as a voluntary action.[137] Johnston obtained similar results at Tiaong in Gardener's civilian-governed Tayabas province. He reported that within days "complete information of all the insurgent bands operating in that entire region was secured and turned over to the different commanding officers where it would be of most service. . . . [and] each surrounding garrison in Tayabas and Laguna was ordered to Tiaong to inform themselves as to the conditions found and to receive instruction as to the methods used in procuring the information and breaking up the organizations."[138] The discovery of organized *insurrecto* support in Tayabas caused Bell to recommend the ports of Tayabas province be closed just as the ports of Laguna and Batangas had been closed on 10 December.[139] The American pressure continued against increasingly smaller and smaller numbers of *insurrectos*.

Finally, on 16 April, Malvar surrendered "without escort, without arms, and without guides."[140] He gave as the reasons for his surrender "the measures of General Bell . . . reconcentration, the complete cleaning up of food supplies outside the towns, and persecution of the insurgent soldier by the people, the search for myself by the people, and the demoralization of my troops."[141] On 6 May Malvar issued his last manifesto, "I proclaim and make known by means of this edict to all concerned that the war carried on against the authority of the Untied States by the Filipino people, has ended."[142] Ten days later in his last telegraphic circular Bell said, "In view of the fact that all insurgents have now surrendered in Batangas and Laguna, it is desired to put a complete end to every war measure heretofore authorized and enforced and to re-establish a feeling of security and tranquility among the people as rapidly as possible."[143] On 23 June control of Batangas province was transferred from military to civilian government.[144]

Well-conceived, carefully planned, vigorously executed, and tightly controlled, Bell's campaign plan worked. Between 1 December 1901 and 30 April 1902, Bell's Third Separate Brigade killed 210 *insurrectos*, wounded 139, and captured 899 along with 629 rifles. During the same time, 2,973 *insurrectos* surrendered with 2,264 firearms.[145] More importantly, it destroyed the linkage between the guerrillas in the field and the infrastructure in the town. This permitted the destruction of the *insurrecto* support system and made the guerrilla units vulnerable to sustained American military action. However, the countryside was devastated. Concentrating the population into makeshift zones of protection for over 4 months created unhealthy conditions and made the transmission of communicable diseases among the populace easier. A higher civilian death rate resulted.[146] For all concerned—civilians, *insurrectos*, and Americans—the campaign in southwestern Luzon proved "by far the longest, most costly, and most difficult pacification campaign in Luzon."[147]

Situation in the Philippines, July 1902

On 4 July 1902, President Roosevelt declared the end of the Philippine Insurrection. He granted amnesty to all Filipinos who took the oath of allegiance and established civil government throughout regions of the archipelago not inhabited by the Moro tribes.[148] On that same day, Roosevelt issued thanks to the US Army for its service in the Philippines (see appendix D). Roosevelt described the 40-month insurrection that had involved virtually the entire US Army and numerous volunteer regiments as a "peculiarly difficult and trying" task. To "crush out a general system of guerrilla warfare conducted among a people speaking unknown tongues, from whom it was almost impossible to obtain the information necessary for successful pursuit or to guard against surprise and ambush" had not been easy.[149] The war in the Philippines was costly to all. Of the 126,500 Americans who served, 4,200 died (a death rate of 32:1,000) and over 2,800 were wounded—a total casualty rate of 5.5 percent. Financial costs totaled over $400 million or 20 times the original purchase price for the Philippines. The *insurrectos* lost 16,000 to 20,000 killed and about 34,000 Filipinos died as a direct result of the war. Another 200,000 noncombatants died in a cholera epidemic at the end of the war. These civilian losses would be equivalent to the United States losing 1 million out of a population of 250 million from war deaths and over 8 million from disease. This little known war was more than an insignificant skirmish for all those involved.[150]

Notes

1.   Quoted in Glenn A. May, *Battle for Batangas: A Philippine Province at War* (New Haven, CT: Yale University Press, 1991), 161.

2.   Brain M. Linn, *The Philippine War, 1899–1902* (Lawrence, KS: University of Kansas Press, 2000), 160–169; May, *Batangas*, 95–126.

3.   Brian M. Linn, *The U.S. Army and Counterinsurgency in the Philippine War, 1899–1902* (Chapel Hill, NC: The University of North Carolina Press, 1989), 122–123.

4.   War Department, Bureau of Insular Affairs, *A Pronouncing Gazetteer and Geographical Dictionary of the Philippine Islands, United States of America, with Maps, Charts, and Illustrations. Also the Law of Civil Government in the Philippine Islands Passed by Congress and Approved by the President July 1, 1902* (Washington, DC: Government Printing Office, 1902), 345–346, 572, 882–883. Hereafter referred to as WD, BIA.

5.   May, *Batangas*, 25. Morbidity in Batangas—37.2:1,000—was greater than twice the morbidity rate in the United States and twice that of Europe. In 1883 and 1889, cholera epidemics raised the rates to 75:1,000 and over 80:1,000. Of the places that kept data at the time, only India, Singapore, and the Philippines competed for the unhealthiest place on earth. Climate, disease, poor sanitation, and nutritional deficiency were all factors in the morbidity rate.

6.   WD, BIA, 344, 571, 882.

7.   Ibid., 344–347, 571–574, 882–885.

8.   Ibid.

9.   Brigadier General James F. Wade quoted in Linn, *U.S. Army*, 120.

10.   May, *Batangas*, 10.

11.   Glenn A. May, "Filipino Resistance to American Occupation: Batangas, 1899–1902," *Pacific Historical Review,* November 1979, 533; WD, BIA, 348–349, 574–575, 885–886.

12.   May, "Filipino Resistance," 533.

13.   May, *Batangas*, 28.

14.   Charles J. Crane, *The Experiences of a Colonel of Infantry* (New York, NY: The Knickerbocker Press, 1923), 335.

15.   May, *Batangas*, 9.

16.   Ibid., 12.

17.   Ibid., 31–34.

18.   John R.M. Taylor, *The Philippine Insurrection Against the United States: A Compilation of Documents with Notes and Introduction, Volume II, May 19, 1898 to July 4, 1902*, vol. II, 23. This is a galley proof of an unpublished War Department manuscript in *History of the Philippine Insurrection against the United States, 1899–1903: and documents relating to the War Department project for publishing the history* (Washington, DC: National Archives, 1968), roll 9. Microfilm. Hereafter referred to as Taylor, USNA.

19.   May, *Batangas*, 61.

20.   For details, see May, *Batangas*, 36–87.

21. Linn, *U.S. Army*, 129.
22. Linn, *Philippine War*, 287; Linn, *U.S. Army*, 129–130.
23. Linn, *U.S. Army*, 131–132; May, *Batangas*, 165, 169–170.
24. Linn, *U.S. Army*, 135–136.
25. May, *Batangas*, 192.
26. Linn, *U.S. Army*, 137.
27. Linn, *Philippine War*, 289.
28. Taylor, USNA, vol. II, 24, roll 9.
29. Quoted in Linn, *U.S. Army*, 135.
30. Lieutenant Colonel Charles J. Crane, 14 November 1900, quoted in Linn, *U.S. Army*, 133.
31. Colonel William E. Birkhimer, 15 July 1900, quoted in Linn, *U.S. Army*, 137–138.
32. Quoted in May, *Batangas*, 166.
33. Major General John C. Bates, born in Missouri in 1842, attended Washington University of St. Louis, first lieutenant 11th Infantry 1861, during the American Civil War served in Army of the Potomac at Antietam, Fredericksburg, Chancellorsville, and Gettysburg, aide to General Meade, captain 1863, brevets to major and lieutenant colonel, 20th Infantry 1866, served on Indian frontier in 20th and 2d Infantry 1866–98, major 1882, lieutenant colonel 1886, colonel 1892, brigadier general volunteers and brigade commander in Cuba 1898, major general volunteers and division commander in Cuba 1898, Philippines 1899, commander 1st Division 1900, commander Department of Southern Luzon 1900–1901, brigadier general February 1901, major general July 1902.
34. WD, BIA, 138–139; Linn, *Philippine War*, 277.
35. Brigadier General Robert H. Hall, graduated West Point 1860, 2d lieutenant 10th Infantry, 20 battles during American Civil War, served in the west, 7 years adjutant of the Military Academy, major 1883, lieutenant colonel 1888, colonel 1893, brigadier general volunteers 1898, commanded 3d Brigade of 2d Division Philippines, 1899.
36. Linn, *U.S. Army*, 123; May, *Batangas*, 134.
37. Allan R. Millett, *The General: Robert L. Bullard and Officership in the United States Army, 1881–1925* (Westport, CT: Greenwood Press, 1975), 137; Linn, *Philippine War*, 286; Linn, *U.S. Army*, 123.
38. Quoted in May, *Batangas*, 133.
39. Ibid., 134.
40. Quoted in Linn, *U.S. Army*, 123.
41. Ibid., 129.
42. Ibid., 123.
43. Ibid., 125.
44. Ibid., 126.
45. Ibid.
46. Linn, *Philippine War*, 289–290.
47. Ibid., 211.
48. Linn, *U.S. Army*, 129.

49. Ibid., 128–129.

50. Millett, 143.

51. James A. LeRoy, *The Americans in the Philippines: A History of the Conquest and First Years of Occupation with an Introductory Account of the Spanish Rule*, 2 vols. (Boston, MA: The Riverside Press Cambridge, 1914), vol. II, 219–221.

52. May, *Batangas*, 137.

53. Ibid., 146.

54. Quoted in May, *Batangas*, 147.

55. Quoted in Linn, *U.S. Army*, 139.

56. Ibid.

57. Ibid., 140.

58. Quoted in May, *Batangas*, 152.

59. May, *Batangas*, 151–152; Linn, *U.S. Army*, 138.

60. Quoted in LeRoy, vol. II, 216.

61. Linn, *U.S. Army*, 143.

62. Telegram, MacArthur to War Department, received 19 September 1900, in US Army, Adjutant General's Office, *Correspondence Relating to the War with Spain and Conditions Growing out of the Same Including the Insurrection in the Philippine Islands and the China Relief Expedition, Between the Adjutant-General of the Army and Military Commanders in the United States, Cuba, Porto Rico, China, and the Philippine Islands from April 15, 1898 to July 30, 1902* (Washington, DC: Government Printing Office, 1902), vol. II, 1211.

63. Linn, *U.S. Army*, 138; William T. Sexton, *Soldiers in the Sun: An Adventure in Imperialism* (Freeport, NY: Books for Libraries Press, 1971), 249–250.

64. May, *Batangas*, 152.

65. Ibid., 150–151.

66. Linn, *U.S. Army*, 131–132; May, *Batangas*, 169–170.

67. Taylor, USNA, vol. II, 53, roll 9.

68. Millett, 148.

69. Linn, *U.S. Army*, 143.

70. Ibid., 127.

71. Ibid., 141.

72. Ibid., 142.

73. Ibid., 146.

74. Taylor, USNA, vol. II, 54, roll 9.

75. *Facts About the Filipinos* in *History of the Philippine Insurrection against the United States, 1899–1903: and documents relating to the War Department project for publishing the history* (Washington, DC: National Archives, 1968), 93–95, roll 8. Microfilm. Hereafter referred to as USNA.

76. Telegram, MacArthur to War Department, received 16 March 1901, US Army, *Correspondence*, vol. II, 1259.

77. Linn, *U.S. Army*, 149–150; May, *Batangas*, 213–216.

78. Linn, *U.S. Army*, 143.

79. Brigadier General Samuel S. Sumner, son of American Civil War major general; 19-year old cavalry second lieutenant 1861, three brevets for bravery during Civil War, captain 1865, Indian campaigns, major 1879, lieutenant colonel 1891, colonel 1896, San Juan Hill Cuba 1898, brigadier general February 1901, commander First District Department of Southern Luzon 1901.

80. Linn, *U.S. Army*, 143; May, *Batangas*, 222–224.

81. Linn, *U.S. Army*, 146.

82. May, *Batangas*, 225.

83. Quoted in *Facts About the Filipinos*, USNA, 112, roll 8.

84. Ibid., 113.

85. Telegram, MacArthur to War Department, received 24 June 1901, US Army, *Correspondence*, vol. II, 1288.

86. Linn, *Philippine War*, 297.

87. Linn, *U.S. Army*, 149.

88. Quoted in May, *Batangas*, 227–228.

89. Ibid., 229.

90. Brian M. Linn, "Intelligence and Low-intensity Conflict in the Philippine War, 1899–1902," *Intelligence and National Security,* January 1991, 102.

91. May, *Batangas*, 226–230.

92. Taylor, USNA, vol. II, 55, roll 9.

93. John M. Gates, *Schoolbooks and Krags: The United States Army in the Philippines, 1898–1902* (Westport, CT: Greenwood Press Inc., 1973), 242.

94. May, *Batangas*, 231–232.

95. Quoted in Linn, *U.S. Army*, 151.

96. Quoted in Linn, "Intelligence," 90.

97. Ibid., 102.

98. Ibid., 103.

99. Quoted in May, *Batangas*, 235.

100. Quoted in Linn, *U.S. Army*, 152.

101. For accounts of the pacification of Samar, see Linn, *Philippine War*, 306–321; Sexton, 268–276; Stuart C. Miller, *"Benevolent Assimilation": The American Conquest of the Philippines, 1899–1903* (New Haven, CT: Yale University Press, 1982), 219–252; Leon Wolfe, *Little Brown Brother: How the United States Purchased and Pacified the Philippine Islands at the Century's Turn* (Garden City, NY: Doubleday and Company, Inc., 1961), 354–359.

102. Telegram, Roosevelt to Chaffee, sent 8 October 1901, US Army, *Correspondence*, vol. II, 1297.

103. John M. Gates, *The U.S. Army and Irregular Warfare*. Chapter V, 3, online, available at http://www.wooster.edu/history/jgates/book-contents.html.

104. May, *Batangas*, 238.

105. Richard E. Welch, *Response to Imperialism: The United States and the Philippine–American War, 1899–1902* (Chapel Hill, NC: The University of North Carolina Press, 1979), 41.

106. War Department, General Orders 148, dated 9 November 1901, US Army, *Correspondence*, vol. II, 1302.

107. War Department, *Annual Report of Major General Adna R. Chaffee, United States Army, Commanding the Division of the Philippines, September 30, 1902* (Manila, PI, 1902), 7. Hereafter referred to as WD, *Annual Report Chaffee.*

108. Taylor, USNA, vol. II, 23, roll 9.

109. Brigadier General James Franklin Bell, born in Kentucky in 1856, West Point graduate 1878, second lieutenant 9th Cavalry 1878, transferred 7th Cavalry 1878, served Fort Buford 1882–86, professor of military science and tactics at Southern Illinois University 1886–89, studied law and admitted to bar, first lieutenant 1890, adjutant 7th Cavalry at Fort Riley 1891–94, aide commander Department of California 1894–97, Fort Apache 1897–98, major of volunteers and engineer officer to VIII Corps 1898, Department of the Pacific chief of military information 1898, captain 1899, major of volunteers 1899 and acting judge advocate 2d Division, colonel of volunteers and commander 36th USV July 1899, Medal of Honor September 1899, brigadier general volunteers December 1899, commanded 4th Brigade of 2d Division 1900, provost marshal of Manila 1900–1901, promoted captain to brigadier general February 1901, commanded 2d District Department of Northern Luzon February 1901, commanded Third Separate Brigade Department of Luzon November 1901–02, commandant Army Service Schools at Fort Leavenworth 1902–06, major general 1907, US Army chief of staff 1906–10, died on Active Duty in 1919.

110. Gates, *Schoolbooks*, 241.

111. WD, *Annual Report Chaffee*, 30–31.

112. Linn, *U.S. Army*, 152.

113. Transcript from meeting 1 December 1901, in Milton F. Davis, compiler. *Telegraphic Circulars and General Orders, Regulating Campaign Against Insurgents and Proclamations and Circular Letters, Relating to Reconstruction after Close of War in the Provinces of Batangas, Laguna and Mindoro, Philippine Islands, Issued by Brigadier General J. Franklin Bell, U.S. Army, Commanding Brigade, from December 1st, 1901, to December 1st, 1902* (Batangas, Batangas Province, PI: Headquarters Third Separate Brigade, December 1902), i–x.

114. US Congress, Senate, *Affairs in the Philippine Islands. Hearings before the Committee on the Philippines of the United States Senate,* General Orders 1, Third Separate Brigade, 3 December 1901 (Senate Document 331, part 2, 57th Congress, 1st Session, 1902), 1642–1643.

115. Ibid., General Orders 2, Third Separate Brigade, 5 December 1901, 1643.

116. Ibid., General Orders 5, Third Separate Brigade, 28 December 1901, 1646.

117. Davis, Telegraphic Circular No. 2, 8 December 1901, 1–2.

118. Ibid., Telegraphic Circular No. 3, 9 December 1901, 2–6.

119. Ibid., Telegraphic Circular No. 5, 13 December 1901, 7–9.

120. Ibid., Telegraphic Circular No. 10, 20 December 1901, 11–12.

121. Ibid., Telegraphic Circular No. 14, 21 December 1901, 13–14.

122. Ibid., Telegraphic Circular No. 18, 23 December 1910, 16–17.

123. Ibid., Telegraphic Circular No. 19, 24 December 1901, 17–18.

124. Ibid., Telegraphic Circular No. 20, 24 December 1901, 19–20.
125. Ibid., Telegraphic Circular No. 21, 24 December 1901, 20–21.
126. Ibid., Telegraphic Circular No. 23, 28 December 1901, 22–23.
127. Ibid., Telegraphic Circular No. 22, 24 December 1901, 21–22.
128. US Congress, *Affairs in the Philippine Islands*, Telegram, Bell to Wheaton, 26 December 1901, 1691.
129. Ibid., Telegram, Bell to Wheaton, 26 December 1901, 1690–1692.
130. May, *Batangas*, 255.
131. Linn, *U.S. Army*, 157.
132. Taylor, USNA, vol. II, 26, roll 9.
133. US Congress, *Affairs in the Philippine Islands*, Telegram, Wheaton to Chaffee, 14 January 1902, 1700.
134. May, "Filipino Resistance," 550.
135. Linn, *U.S. Army*, 158.
136. Davis, Telegraph, Bell to All Station Commanders, 16 January 1902, 33–34.
137. Linn, *U.S. Army,* 156.
138. Linn, "Intelligence," 107.
139. Taylor, USNA, vol. II, 26, roll 9.
140. Russell Roth, *Muddy Glory: America's 'Indian Wars' in the Philippines, 1899–1935* (W. Hanover, MA: The Christopher Publishing House, 1981), 88.
141. Linn, *U.S. Army*, 159.
142. Roth, 88.
143. Davis, Telegraphic Circular No. 38, 16 May 1902, 32.
144. WD, *Annual Report Chaffee*, 12.
145. Linn, *U.S. Army*, 159.
146. Glenn A. May, "The 'Zones' of Batangas," *Philippine Studies* 29, 1981, 95.
147. Linn, *U.S. Army*, 160.
148. Sexton, 284. Pacification of the Moros in the southern Philippines would take several years.
149. Headquarters of the Army, General Orders No. 66, 4 July 1902, US Army, *Correspondence*, vol. II, 1352.
150. Welch, 42. Gates, *US Army and Irregular Warfare*, chapter 3, 1. The cholera epidemic appears to have originated in India and reached Manila in March 1902. It took about 2 months for it to break out in Batangas province. See John M. Gates, "War-Related Deaths in the Philippines, 1898–1902," *Pacific Historical Review,* November 1983, 375–376.

Chapter 4

Observations

> The condition of our military forces there might be compared to that of a blind giant. The troops were more than able to annihilate, to completely smash anything that could be brought against them in the shape of military force on the part of the insurgents; but it was almost impossible to get information in regard to those people. The natives were afraid to give us any information because if they did they were boloed. . . . It was a very embarrassing situation. . . . the island was practically in the possession of a blind giant; strong, but unable to see where to strike.
>
> Colonel Arthur L. Wagner[1]

The metaphor of the US Army in the Philippines as a blind giant aptly describes most armies that face armed resistance in an occupied alien country. Then, as now, being blind creates a "very embarrassing situation." Overcoming language and cultural barriers proved a necessity for the Americans to begin to comprehend their situation. At a minimum, it required a willingness by some of the population to work with the Americans and a willingness by the Americans to trust some of the natives. This took time to develop. Where either was missing, the Americans remained blind. In February 1899, the month war began in the Philippines, Rudyard Kipling penned a description of what he thought Americans needed to understand about their undertaking in the Philippines in a poem:

The White Man's Burden[2]

The United States and the Philippine Islands

Take up the White Man's burden—
  Send forth the best ye breed—
Go bind your sons to exile
  To serve your captives' need;
To wait in heavy harness,
  On fluttered folk and wild—
Your new-caught, sullen peoples,
  Half-devil and half-child.

Take up the White Man's burden—
  In patience to abide,

To veil the threat of terror
    And check the show of pride;
By open speech and simple,
    An hundred times made plain
To seek another's profit,
    And work another's gain.

Take up the White Man's burden—
    The savage wars of peace—
Fill full the mouth of Famine
    And bid the sickness cease;
And when your goal is nearest
    The end for others sought,
Watch sloth and heathen Folly
Bring all your hopes to nought.

Take up the White Man's burden—
    No tawdry rule of kings,
But toil of serf and sweeper—
    The tale of common things.
The ports ye shall not enter,
    The roads ye shall not tread,
Go mark them with your living,
    And mark them with your dead.

Take up the White Man's burden—
    And reap his old reward:
The blame of those ye better,
    The hate of those ye guard—
The cry of hosts ye humour
    (Ah, slowly!) toward the light—
"Why brought he us from bondage,
    Our loved Egyptian night?"

Take up the White Man's burden—
    Ye dare not stoop to less—
Nor call too loud on Freedom
    To cloke your weariness;
By all ye cry or whisper,
    By all ye leave or do,
The silent, sullen peoples
    Shall weigh your gods and you.

Take up the White Man's burden—
    Have done with childish days—

The lightly proferred laurel,
The easy, ungrudged praise.
Comes now, to search your manhood
Through all the thankless years
Cold, edged with dear-bought wisdom,
The judgment of your peers!

The burden of occupation and colonial rule described by Kipling had no simple, short-term, or doctrinal solution. In the Philippines, a solution required an understanding of the local situation to develop effective measures for gaining support of the population and for destroying the armed *insurrectos*. That proved no easy task.

After the war, the American Army remained blind about its 40-month Philippine experience. Brigadier General James L. Collins, Jr., a former Army chief of military history, believed that if there had been organized material on the Philippine Insurrection, "we could have saved ourselves a good deal of time and effort in Vietnam."[3] In fact, Captain John R.M. Taylor, 14th Infantry, had written a five-volume official history on the Philippine experience—two volumes of history and three volumes of documents. Taylor finished a review of the galley proofs of *The Philippine Insurrection Against the United States: A Compilation of Documents with Notes and Introduction* in 1906. However, the Bureau of Insular Affairs failed to publish it for political reasons.[4] Other than William T. Sexton's pre-World War II *Soldiers in the Sun* and John M. Gates' *Schoolbooks and Krags: The United States Army in the Philippines, 1898–1902* (1973), the few works on the Philippine War viewed it through the prism of Vietnam. Recently, historian Brian M. Linn has enhanced our understanding of the war in the Philippines through meticulous research and publication of articles and two outstanding books—*The U.S. Army and Counterinsurgency in the Philippine War, 1899–1902* (1989) and *The Philippine War, 1899–1902* (2000). Linn's works, supplemented by regional studies such as Glenn A. May's *Battle for Batangas: A Philippine Province at War* (1991), help fill the blind spot about the war in the Philippines.

Before comparing the two case studies—the Ilocos region and the Tagalog provinces in Second District, Department of Southern Luzon—it is important to remember the following. First, only 43 of 77 provinces in the Philippines resisted American occupation.[5] This meant from the beginning that the policy of benevolent assimilation or attraction applied in many parts of the Philippines. It worked in the regions without *insurrectos*. At any rate, in *insurrecto* areas, the policy of attraction proved inadequate without an accompanying policy of coercion to break the linkage between the *insurrecto* support base of the towns and the guerrillas in the field. Although many commanders recommended a harsher policy, Major General MacArthur did not declare martial law under General Orders 100 (appendix B) or establish firmer measures until December 1900. Even then, the understanding of his intent and the support for his programs varied among commanders. Second, these two military districts, comprised of seven provinces, were the most difficult to pacify on Luzon. The decentralized nature of the resistance and the regional differences in the Philippines, almost by definition, made each *insurrecto* challenge and each American response dependent on local conditions. Because no single, simple solution existed to solve the numerous local issues generated by the war, local leaders on both sides played a critical role in its outcome. Third, both case studies presented the perspective of the district commander by focusing on his understanding of the situation, his interaction with superiors and subordinates, and his effectiveness against his adversaries—military and civilian.

Center of Gravity—Filipinos

Reinforced by cultural, social, economic, and political ties, the control of the population rested firmly in the hands of the local elite. As long as the elite provided support—recruits, supplies, intelligence, taxes—the guerrillas were not destroyed. Local militias in each town and most barrios controlled the population merely by their presence. Guerrilla units might be dispersed, but were almost never destroyed. Recruits from the towns filled the losses. In both districts, the population was generally homogenous, Ilocano or Tagalog, providing few opportunities for the Americans to employ minority groups in a divide-and-conquer strategy. With over a year of local rule after the overthrow of the Spanish and before the Americans arrived, the population of both regions, primarily through their ruling elite, supported Filipino rule to foreign occupation. Language and cultural differences permeated all interaction with the Americans. Taylor emphasized this difficulty when he wrote:

> Between the Malays of the Philippines and the American differences in manner of life and manner of thought will probably always run like a deep river, however often it may be bridged by a common education and by community of interest and in spite of the fact that the leaders among them have in the past looked for guidance to Europe and not Asia. . . . government has always been direct and personal; the ruler has always been considered rather the head of a family than the general manager of a corporation; and the Filipinos are Asiatics.[6]

Coercion and terror provided a credible deterrent to those who considered cooperating with the Americans. Nevertheless, the bottom line was that the *insurrectos* provided better security and a greater threat of harm than the Americans. In both case studies, the population followed the lead of the elite. When the elite faltered, support for the guerrillas dropped and some natives cooperated with the Americans. The Tagalog elite, long the cadre of revolution in southern Luzon, proved more dedicated to the *insurrecto* cause than the Ilocano elite. In both regions, after the surrender of the major guerrilla leaders, the local elite quickly accommodated itself to the Americans.[7]

Antagonists—Filipino *Insurrectos*

Following the directives of Aguinaldo's government, the military commanders in the Ilocos and the Tagalog provinces organized regional military and local militia forces based on the towns. The local governments raised, housed, supplied, and maintained these units. Each of these efforts was decentralized and thus had a local and regional flavor. As long as the linkage between the guerrillas in the field and the support infrastructure in the towns existed, the guerrillas proved almost impossible to destroy. By avoiding combat with American units, the guerrillas were generally immune to American counterguerrilla efforts. Guerrilla leaders, selected not for their military skill but for their personal, family, and business ties to the local elite, maintained this link to their support infrastructure. Adopting guerrilla warfare as a strategy of last resort, Aguinaldo held out the possibility not of victory, but of wearing down the Americans and the election of a US president who supported Philippine independence. When President McKinley was re-elected in 1900, almost immediately in the Ilocos militias began to surrender. The activities of the Federal Party, in conjunction with MacArthur's martial law and other measures, increased the strain on both the infrastructure in the towns and the guerrillas in the field. In the spring of 1900 when the capture of Aguinaldo followed the surrender of Lieutenant General Trias, their direct appeals to the *insurrecto* leaders led to the surrender of all the major leaders in the Ilocos and negotiations with Brigadier General Cailles in the south. By the summer of 1901, only Brigadier General Malvar continued to resist on Luzon. Many of the wartime commanders became leaders in the American government after the insurrection.[8]

Protagonists—American Army

American troops—with an average strength of 40,000 during the war—were always insufficient in number to garrison all the towns and to conduct aggressive counterguerrilla operations. Initially, most units remained in the same province for over a year; many remained in the same town. This created familiarity with the local leaders and local conditions. Even so, armed with the confidence, can-do attitude, racism, and cultural insensitivity of Americans of that time, soldiers and commanders found themselves blind in an alien and hostile environment where—

> Few understood the local dialects or Spanish and they were thus dependent on unreliable translators of dubious loyalty. The soldiers had little respect for native culture or society; even those with the highest motives and best intentions sought to make over the Filipinos into little brown Americans. Often referring to their enemy as *ladrones* or *insurrectos* (insurrectionists), they failed to detect the Filipinos' passionate and often semi-mystical desire for independence. Lacking any empathy for indigenous traditions and customs, Americans interpreted all events in a narrow ethnocentric framework. Filipino devoutness was dismissed as superstitions, Filipino sports were banned as barbaric, Filipino emphasis on family connections was slighted in the interest of efficiency, and Filipino politeness and courtesy, manifest often in the desire to put information in the best possible light, was interpreted as dishonesty or shiftiness.[9]

The initial military response was to focus on the security problem—the armed *insurrectos*. By the summer of 1900, the Americans in La Union province had learned of the relationship between the guerrilla units in the field and their infrastructure in the towns, as well as the value of native auxiliaries. Still, it took MacArthur's campaign in December 1900 to provide the impetus and tools needed to attack that linkage using martial law, provost courts, imprisonments, native auxiliaries, and intelligence-driven attacks on the support infrastructure of the towns and at the same time push the guerrillas away from the towns by military operations. MacArthur's program came after repeated calls for harsher measures from Brigadier General Young, Major General Wheaton, and others. By April 1901 this military program, combined with efforts by the Federal Party and the appeal of Aguinaldo to accept American rule, resulted in the surrender of Tinio, Juan Villamor, and Father Aglipay, ending the pacification of the Ilocos. In the Tagalog provinces, the focus of department and district commanders remained on counterguerrilla operations, not the destruction of the infrastructure. After the general collapse of the *insurrecto* movement throughout the Philippines by the summer of 1901, American Army troop strength was reduced by about a third and troops were concentrated in troublesome regions. The infrastructure in the Tagalog region was never attacked until Brigadier General Bell's pacification of Batangas began in December 1901.

Insights of the American Counterinsurgency in the Philippines

The American approach to pacification evolved during the war. President McKinley's policy of benevolent assimilation initially focused the military on civil-military actions to improve the lives of the Filipinos—Governor Taft's "little brown brothers." In fact, most of what the Americans offered, short of independence, coincided with or exceeded the programs of the pre-war Filipino reformers and revolutionaries. At the end of hostilities from the American perspective and the beginning of guerrilla warfare from the *insurrecto* perspective in late 1899 and early 1900, the American Army initially began a bottom-up civil-military effort to establish local governments and to improve local educational, sanitary, and governmental functions. When the guerrilla or ladrone problem persisted, the American Army sought to do what it was trained to do—destroy the armed *insurrectos*. The civil-military effort and destroying the guerrillas proved more difficult than anticipated in both case studies. When an understanding of the relationship between the guerrillas in the field and the infrastructure in the towns became known and martial law (General Orders 100) and new policies were established by MacArthur at the end of 1900, the focus shifted in the Ilocos to separating the guerrillas from the towns and destroying both the guerrilla bands and the infrastructure in the towns. With the techniques learned in La Union province, the reinforcements provided by Wheaton, the assistance of local auxiliaries, the leadership of Young and Bell, and the actions of provincial and post commanders, the destruction of the infrastructure and the guerrilla units in the Ilocos was well underway when resistance ended after the major guerrilla leaders surrendered. In the Tagalog region, this final phase did not occur until Bell's pacification campaign in 1901–02. These efforts took time to develop, and they were affected by nonmilitary events—the American presidential election, the work of the Federal Party, and the surrender and appeals of major *insurrecto* leaders.

Nonmilitary factors proved as important as military operations. First, the geography of the archipelago made external resupply of the *insurrectos* difficult and denied them a nearby safe haven or sanctuary. The American naval blockade made *insurrecto* resupply and coordination within and outside the archipelago difficult. Combined with the restriction on firearms during the prewar Spanish period, a finite number of weapons limited the *insurrecto* threat and made the capture of firearms a metric of

117

success in the end. Second, support in the United States for the effort in the Philippines remained strong throughout the war. However, political opposition in America stiffened the *insurrecto* resolve in their hope for the election of Democratic candidate William Jennings Bryan in 1900 who they believed would grant independence to the Philippines. The re-election of President McKinley undercut this *insurrecto* strategy and demoralized many *insurrecto* supporters. Third, the activities of the Filipino Federal Party as a pro-American alternative to the *insurrectos* were important in undercutting the support for the *insurrectos* and in negotiating the surrender of major *insurrecto* leaders. Finally, the willingness and ability to get captured and surrendered leaders—particularly Aguinaldo and Trias—to issue proclamations supporting the American occupation and encouraging their followers to surrender proved critical in the general collapse of the insurrection on Luzon by mid-1901.

Understanding the local situation was the critical problem faced by American commanders. Without the language skills or an appreciation of the need for cultural understanding, the Americans were, in Wagner's words, blind. Naturally, they sought to apply American solutions to what they considered Filipino problems. In his 1902 annual report, Chaffee wrote of the need for language skills:

> An important duty as yet not taken seriously by the officers of the Army serving in the Division, but which ought not be longer neglected if they would meet to the full the demands which the situation requires and may be reasonably expected of them as enhancing the efficiency when serving here, is the acquirement of a workable knowledge, both oral and written, of the native dialect where stationed. . . . I believe that the interests of the government are deeply involved in this matter. . . . I recommend . . . a bonus of two hundred dollars to each officer and intelligent enlisted man who shall attain a state of proficiency in a native dialect, and one hundred dollars additional for proficiency in Spanish.[10]

Long-term garrisoning of towns with American troops provided post commanders the opportunity to gain an understanding of their situation and their locale. It provided the opportunity to identify locals who might be willing to work with the Americans. In many parts of the Philippines, Filipinos worked with the Americans. The Macabebes served effectively as part of Major General Otis's forces in the fall of 1899. But this willingness to work with the Americans did not generally exist in the Ilocos or the Tagalog regions. The chance arrest of the leader of the *Guardia de Honor* provided the Americans in the Ilocos both an understanding of the *insurrecto* intent and structure and a source of local auxiliaries better equipped to work among the population than the Americans were. Reliable intelligence and native forces with local knowledge were essential for the Americans to understand and to destroy the *insurrectos* in La Union province. When Colonel Duvall created a regimental or provincial intelligence section, he was able to develop actionable intelligence and attack local threats. Within a short time, the province was pacified by taking control of the towns and isolating the guerrilla forces from their support system. Use of the *Guardia*, and later the Igorots in southern Ilocos Sur province, and the development of provincial and district intelligence sections facilitated pacification operations in other parts of the First District. In the Tagalog region, the American department and district commanders resisted the use of native troops. They did not create a district or lower-level intelligence section until September 1901. Recruiting Tagalogs may have been difficult, but failure to trust the natives and the unwillingness to work with what Otis called religious fanatics was the basic American problem. The "need for local auxiliaries, even if it means embracing rather unsavory allies" to gain situational awareness, reliable intelligence, and forces capable of working directly with the local populace appeared not to have been understood or accepted by the department or district commanders in the Tagalog provinces until Bell arrived.[11]

Finding a solution to the local insurrecto challenge varied from place to place, but the basic requirement became the separation of the guerrillas in the field from their support structure in the towns. In both the Ilocano and the Tagalog provinces, the policy of attraction with local government, police, education, and sanitation programs proved inadequate to this challenge. Attraction, without sanctions, did not work. Even after the relationship between the local elite in the towns and the guerrilla leaders in the field become known, attempts by post, district, and department commanders to reconcile the legal constraints of attraction with the need to deal directly with noncombatants who supported the *insurrectos* was not resolved in an effective manner until MacArthur's campaign to separate the guerrillas from the towns. MacArthur provided the legal tools—martial law, provost courts, revised rules of evidence, and imprisonment for the duration—for those commanders who understood the importance of destroying the infrastructure and who had a willingness to take on this difficult task. Encouraged by Young and Bell, the commanders in the Ilocos—post, province, and district—took the fight to the guerrillas in the field and to the infrastructure in the towns. This two-pronged attack, combined with the presidential election, the efforts of the Federal Party, and the surrender and capture of major *insurrecto* leaders ended resistance in the Ilocos in April 1901. In fact, the insurrection on Luzon collapsed by the summer of 1901 except in the Tagalog provinces where a direct focused attack on the infrastructure had not occurred. Lack of support for certain programs and lack of understanding of the importance or the manner in which to attack the infrastructure by department, district, and post commanders failed to separate the towns from the guerrillas. Bell, stressing the legality of his actions to his subordinates by repeated references to articles of General Orders 100 first employed in the American Civil War some 35 to 40 years earlier, would force the Tagalog populace to choose between the Americans and the *insurrectos*. As a Philippine veteran noted, "The American soldier in officially sanctioned wrath is a thing so ugly and dangerous that it would take a Kipling to describe him."[12] Bell was faced with a "classic Hobson's choice" in which "A commander committed to quick victory often had to order actions that others might deem inhumane; one committed to upholding certain standards of military behavior, on the other hand, had to be willing to endure the consequences of continued stalemate."[13] With legal backgrounds, Otis, MacArthur, and Bell all sought effective but legal means for ending the insurrection. Ultimately, that required making the supporters of the guerrillas accountable for their roles in prolonging hostilities. Today many of the measures undertaken may appear harsh, but they were legal at the time and they were effective. When the *insurrectos* were defeated and security established, attraction then became the most effective tool of pacification throughout the archipelago.

Understanding the insurrectos and having appropriate tools to attack required a willingness at the local level to attack that threat in an effective manner. This made a decentralized, locally-developed response necessary—just as the *insurrectos* had discovered when they went to guerrilla warfare. To work well, decentralized military operations required regimental commanders and below who were willing and able to learn by trial and error by adjusting to local conditions. From senior officers, it required a willingness to listen and to support their commanders in the provinces and in the towns. Senior commanders familiar with General Orders 100 from the American Civil War brought their experiences to the Philippines. From the Indian Wars, senior commanders brought a willingness to conduct dispersed, small-unit operations that relied on the initiative, adaptability, and aggressiveness of their subordinates.[14] In the Ilocos, Wheaton, Young, and Bell were strong advocates for their subordinates. Wheaton often forwarded reports from his post commanders to the division commander in Manila. Young repeatedly supported both

Duvall and Lieutenant Colonel Howze—two of his most innovative and effective regimental commanders—when their actions were questioned by higher headquarters. Department and district commanders in the Tagalog provinces had decentralized their operations, but they were not as supportive or responsive to suggestions from their subordinates as indicated by Major Steele's attempts to establish civil government in Lucban and Tayabas provinces. For effective commanders, guidance from the Division of the Philippines was treated as guidance—not as directive. In the field, the key remained "the ability of officers to construct pragmatic pacification policies designed to meet the realities of the guerrilla war in their towns, provinces and districts."[15] Local commanders adopted appropriate measures to the conditions as constrained or supported by their chain of command. Unconditional support of subordinates was the norm in the Ilocos. In comparison, until Bell's campaign, support for subordinate recommendations was less common in the Tagalog region.

Just as many Americans did not initially understand the relationship between the guerrilla bands and the towns, many commanders found it frustrating to attempt to pursue civil affairs work in pursuit of the policy of attraction while chasing armed insurrectos and trying to create a secure environment. Some, such as Otis, MacArthur, and Gardener were strong advocates of the policy of attraction. Others, such as Bates, Wade, and Young were strong advocates of the policy of coercion. MacArthur and Bell eventually came to understood that attraction was necessary in the long term, but destruction of the guerrillas and their infrastructure was required first. One historian observed: "Within the army and the American government there was no group of 'experts' with preconceived ideas on how to run a colonial government, and the very absence of this group made possible the successful pragmatic approach that the Americans did use."[16] Another suggested: "Indeed, the key to the Army's success was its lack of adherence to rigid doctrines or theories and the willingness of its officers to experiment with novel pacification schemes."[17] Today, given a highly-trained professionalized military and its institutional reliance on military doctrine, one wonders if preconceived ideas are likely to lead to a doctrinal approach for a problem not addressed in doctrine or to a pragmatic approach for a unique problem.

A comparison of pacification of the Ilocos and the Tagalog provinces has identified similarities and differences in approach and in result. A survey of other districts and different levels of command would provide additional insights and demonstrate a variety of approaches—successful and unsuccessful—to the challenges of pacification. As historian John Gates noted:

The American pacification campaign in the Philippines was important. An example of the successful evolution of a counter-guerrilla operation leading to the effective occupation of a vast and hostile territory, it was developed empirically with no pre-existing doctrine from which to draw. The army's approach to the problem was notable for its diversity, including widespread civil affairs efforts, excellent propaganda, well-planned and executed military operations, effective isolation of the guerrilla, protection of the population, and the involvement of the inhabitants in programs designed for their own protection and the eventual establishment of peace.[18]

The study of the war in the Philippines "can offer great insight into the complexities of localized guerrilla war and indigenous resistance to foreign control. As the most successful counterinsurgency campaign in US history, it is the logical starting point for the systematic examination of military intervention, civic action, and pacification operations."[19] Perhaps, such a systematic examination might reduce our chances of being caught blind again in a similar embarrassing situation.

Notes

1. Testimony of Colonel Arthur L. Wagner, US Congress, Senate, *Affairs in the Philippine Islands. Hearings before the Committee on the Philippines of the United States Senate* (Senate Document 331, part 3, 57th Congress, 1st Session, 1902), 2850–2851.

2. Rudyard Kipling, "The White Man's Burden," online at http://www.fordham.edu/halsall/mod/Kipling.html.

3. John M. Gates, "The Official Historian and the Well-Placed Critic: James A. LeRoy's Assessment of John R.M. Taylor's *The Philippine Insurrection Against the United States*," *The Public Historian,* Summer 1985, 57.

4. For details see Gates, "Official Historian," 57–67; John T. Farrell, "An Abandoned Approach to Philippine History: John R.M. Taylor and the Philippine Insurrection Records," *The Catholic Historical Review,* January 1954, 385–407; "Introduction" in US National Archives, *History of the Philippine Insurrection against the United States, 1899–1903: and documents relating to the War Department project for publishing the history* (Washington, DC: National Archives, 1968), ii–xvi, roll 1. Microfilm. Hereafter referred to as USNA.

5. Brian M. Linn, *The Philippine War, 1899–1902* (Lawrence, KS: University of Kansas Press, 2000), 185.

6. John R.M. Taylor, *The Philippine Insurrection Against the United States: A Compilation of Documents with Notes and Introduction, Volume II, May 19, 1898 to July 4, 1902,* vol. II, 58. This is a galley proof of an unpublished War Department manuscript in *History of the Philippine Insurrection against the United States, 1899–1903: and documents relating to the War Department project for publishing the history* (Washington, DC: National Archives, 1968), roll 9. Microfilm. Hereafter referred to as Taylor, USNA.

7. Glenn A. May, *Battle for Batangas: A Philippine Province at War* (New Haven, CT: Yale University Press, 1991), 275.

8. Ibid., 278.

9. Brian M. Linn, "Intelligence and Low-intensity Conflict in the Philippine War, 1899–1902," *Intelligence and National Security,* January 1991, 94–95.

10. War Department, *Annual Report of Major General Adna R. Chaffee, United States Army, Commanding the Division of the Philippines, September 30, 1902* (Manila, PI, 1902), 34.

11. Brian M. Linn, "The US Army and Nation Building and Pacification in the Philippines," in *Armed Diplomacy: Two Centuries of American Campaigning* (Fort Leavenworth, KS: Combat Studies Institute Press, 2003), 87.

12. Quoted in Leon Wolfe, *Little Brown Brother: How the United States Purchased and Pacified the Philippine Islands at the Century's Turn* (Garden City, NY: Doubleday and Company, Inc., 1961), 359.

13. May, *Batangas,* 229.

14. Andrew J. Birtle, *US Army Counterinsurgency and Contingency Operations Doctrine, 1860–1941* (Washington, DC: US Army Center of Military History, 1998), 112–113.

15. Brian M. Linn, *The U.S. Army and Counterinsurgency in the Philippine War, 1899–1902* (Chapel Hill, NC: The University of North Carolina Press, 1989), 168–169.

16. John M. Gates, *Schoolbooks and Krags: The United States Army in the Philippines, 1898–1902* (Westport, CT: Greenwood Press Inc., 1973), 285.

17. Linn, *U.S. Army*, 169.

18. Gates, *Schoolbooks*, 290.

19. Linn, *Philippine War*, 328.

Bibliography

Primary Sources

Blount, James H. *The American Occupation of the Philippines, 1898–1912*. New York, NY: G.P. Putnam's Sons, 1912.

Crane, Charles J. *The Experiences of a Colonel of Infantry*. New York, NY: The Knickerbocker Press, 1923.

Davis, Milton F., compiler. *Telegraphic Circulars and General Orders, Regulating Campaign Against Insurgents and Proclamations and Circular Letters, Relating to Reconstruction after Close of War in the Provinces of Batangas, Laguna and Mindoro, Philippine Islands, Issued by Brigadier General J. Franklin Bell, U.S. Army, Commanding Brigade, from December 1st, 1901, to December 1st, 1902*. Batangas, Batangas Province, PI: Headquarters Third Separate Brigade, December 1902.

Elliott, Charles B. *The Philippines: To the End of the Military Regime*. Indianapolis, IN: Bobbs-Merrill, 1917.

LeRoy, James A. *The Americans in the Philippines: A History of the Conquest and First Years of Occupation with an Introductory Account of the Spanish Rule*. 2 vols. Boston, MA: The Riverside Press Cambridge, 1914.

US Army. Adjutant General's Office. *Correspondence Relating to the War with Spain and Conditions Growing out of the Same Including the Insurrection in the Philippine Islands and the China Relief Expedition, Between the Adjutant-General of the Army and Military Commanders in the United States, Cuba, Porto Rico, China, and the Philippine Islands from April 15, 1898 to July 30, 1902*. 2 vols. Washington, DC: Government Printing Office, 1902.

US Congress. Senate. *Affairs in the Philippine Islands. Hearings before the Committee on the Philippines of the United States Senate*. Senate Document 331, 3 parts, 57th Congress, 1st Session, 1902.

_____. *The People of the Philippines. Letter from the Secretary of War Transmitting an Article on the People of the Philippines Compiled in the Division of Insular Affairs of the War Department*. Senate Document 218, 56th Congress, 2d Session, 1901.

US National Archives. *History of the Philippine Insurrection against the United States, 1899–1903: and documents relating to the War Department project for publishing the history*. Washington, DC: National Archives, 1968. Microfilm.

Verea, F.G. *Guide for the Americans in the Philippines*. Translated by F.C. Fisher. Manila: n.p., 1899.

War Department. *Annual Report of Major General Adna R. Chaffee, United States Army, Commanding the Division of the Philippines, September 30, 1902*. Manila, PI, 1902.

_____. *Annual Report of Major General Arthur MacArthur, US Army, Commanding, Division of the Philippines, Military Governor in the Philippine Islands*. Manila, PI, 1901.

War Department. Bureau of Insular Affairs. *A Pronouncing Gazetteer and Geographical Dictionary of the Philippine Islands, United States of America, with Maps, Charts, and Illustrations. Also the Law of Civil Government in the Philippine Islands Passed by Congress and Approved by the President July 1, 1902*. Washington, DC: Government Printing Office, 1902.

Secondary Sources

Books

Birtle, Andrew J. *US Army Counterinsurgency and Contingency Operations Doctrine, 1860–1941*. Washington, DC: US Army Center of Military History, 1998.

Coates, Stephen D. *Gathering at the Golden Gate: Mobilizing for War in the Philippines, 1898*. Fort Leavenworth, KS: Combat Studies Institute Press, 2006.

Cosmas, Graham A. *An Army for Empire: The United States Army in the Spanish–American War*. Shippensburg, PA: White Mane Publishing Company, Inc., 1994.

Dolan, Ronald E., ed. *Philippines: A Country Study*. Washington, DC: Federal Research Division, Library of Congress, 1991.

Gates, John M. *Schoolbooks and Krags: The United States Army in the Philippines, 1898–1902*. Westport, CT: Greenwood Press Inc., 1973.

Linn, Brian M. *The Philippine War, 1899–1902*. Lawrence, KS: University of Kansas Press, 2000.

_____. *The U.S. Army and Counterinsurgency in the Philippine War, 1899–1902*. Chapel Hill, NC: The University of North Carolina Press, 1989.

May, Glenn A. *Battle for Batangas: A Philippine Province at War*. New Haven, CT: Yale University Press, 1991.

_____. *Social Engineering in the Philippines: The Aims, Execution, and Impact of American Colonial Policy, 1900–1913*. Westport, CT: Greenwood Press, 1980.

Miller, Stuart C. *"Benevolent Assimilation": The American Conquest of the Philippines, 1899–1903*. New Haven, CT: Yale University Press, 1982.

Millett, Allan R. *The General: Robert L. Bullard and Officership in the United States Army, 1881–1925*. Westport, CT: Greenwood Press, 1975.

Millett, Allan R., and Peter Maslowski. *For the Common Defense: A Military History of the United States of America*. New York, NY: The Free Press, 1994.

Millis, Walter. *The Martial Spirit: A Study of Our War with Spain*. New York, NY: Viking Press, 1965.

Ochosa, Orlino A. *The Tinio Brigade: Anti-American Resistance in the Ilocos Provinces, 1899–1901*. Quezon City, PI: New Day Publishers, 1989.

Owen, Norman G., ed. *Compadre Colonialism: Studies on the Philippines under American Rule*. Ann Arbor, MI: Center for South and Southeast Studies, The University of Michigan, 1971.

Roth, Russell. *Muddy Glory: America's 'Indian Wars' in the Philippines, 1899–1935*. W. Hanover, MA: The Christopher Publishing House, 1981.

Scott, William H. *Ilocano Responses to American Aggression 1900–1901*. Quezon City, PI: New Day Publishers, 1986.

Sexton, William T. *Soldiers in the Sun: An Adventure in Imperialism*. Freeport, NY: Books for Libraries Press, 1971.

Silbey, David J. *A War of Frontier and Empire: The Philippine–American War, 1899–1902*. New York, NY: Hill and Wang, 2007.

Trask, David F. *The War with Spain in 1898*. New York, NY: MacMillan Publishing Company, Inc., 1981.

Welch, Richard E. *Response to Imperialism: The United States and the Philippine–American War, 1899–1902*. Chapel Hill, NC: The University of North Carolina Press, 1979.

Wolfe, Leon. *Little Brown Brother: How the United States Purchased and Pacified the Philippine Islands at the Century's Turn*. Garden City, NY: Double and Company, Inc., 1961.

Young, Kenneth R. *The General's General: The Life and Times of Arthur MacArthur*. Boulder, CO: Westview Press, 1994.

Articles

Berthoff, Rowland T. "Taft and MacArthur, 1900–1901: A Study in Civil-Military Relations." *World Politics*, January 1953, 196–213.

Burdett, Thomas F. "A New Evaluation of General Otis' Leadership in the Philippines." *Military Review*, January 1975, 79–87.

Coffman, Edward M. "Batson of the Philippine Scouts." *Parameters* 3, 1977, 68–72.

Farrell, John T. "An Abandoned Approach to Philippine History: John R.M. Taylor and the Philippine Insurrection Records." *The Catholic Historical Review*, January 1954, 385–407.

Gates, John M. "The Official Historian and the Well-Placed Critic: James A. LeRoy's Assessment of John R.M. Taylor's *The Philippine Insurrection Against the United States*." *The Public Historian*, Summer 1985, 57–67.

_____. "The Pacification of the Philippines, 1898–1902," in *The American Military and the Far East: Proceedings of the Ninth Military History Symposium United States Air Force Academy, 1–3 October 1980*, edited by Joe C. Dixon. Washington, DC: United States Air Force Academy and Office of Air Force History, 1980.

_____. "War-Related Deaths in the Philippines, 1898–1902." *Pacific Historical Review*, November 1983, 367–378.

Linn, Brian M. "Intelligence and Low-intensity Conflict in the Philippine War, 1899–1902." *Intelligence and National Security*, January 1991, 90–114.

_____. "Pacification in Northwestern Luzon: An American Regiment in the Philippine–American War, 1899–1901." *Pilipinas* 3, December 1982, 14–25.

_____. "Provincial Pacification in the Philippines, 1900–1901: The First District Department of Northern Luzon." *Military Affairs,* April 1987, 62–66.

_____. "The US Army and Nation Building and Pacification in the Philippines," in *Armed Diplomacy: Two Centuries of American Campaigning.* Fort Leavenworth, KS: Combat Studies Institute Press, 2003.

May, Glenn A. "Filipino Resistance to American Occupation: Batangas, 1899–1902." *Pacific Historical Review,* November 1979, 531–556.

_____. "The 'Zones' of Batangas." *Philippine Studies* 29, 1981, 89–103.

Welch, Richard E. "American Atrocities in the Philippines: The Indictment and the Response." *Pacific Historical Review,* May 1974, 233–253.

Internet Sources

Gates, John M. *The U.S. Army and Irregular Warfare.* Online. Available at http://www.wooster.edu/history/jgates/book-contents.html, accessed July 2007.

Kipling, Rudyard. "The White Man's Burden." Online. Available at http://www.fordham.edu/halsall/mod/Kipling.html, accessed July 2007.

Linn, Brian M. "The Impact of the Imperial Wars (1898–1907) on the U.S. Army." Heritage Lecture No. 908. Delivered 18 June 2005. Published 14 November 2005. Online. Available at http://www.heritage.org/Research/NationalSecurity/hl908.cfm, accessed July 2007.

War Department. "General Orders No. 100, Instructions for the Government of Armies of the United States in the Field, 24 April 1863." Online. Available at http://www.usregulars.com/Lieber.html, accessed 30 May 2007.

Appendix A

Chronology

1896

Aug	Bonifacio led *Katipunan* revolt

1897

May	Bonifacio executed Aguinaldo became leader of *Katipunan*
Dec	Pact of Biyak-na-Bato Aguinaldo exiled to Hong Kong

1898

Mar	Revolt at Candon in Ilocos Sur province suppressed by Spanish forces
25 Apr	United States declared war on Spain
Apr–May	War Department raised state volunteer regiments and increased Regular Army
1 May	Battle of Manila Bay; Commodore Dewey sank Spanish fleet
May	Major General Merritt assigned command of VIII Corps Aguinaldo returned to Philippines Spanish garrison in Manila besieged by Aguinaldo's forces
Jun	Aguinaldo consolidated power by assuming command of revolutionary movement, by establishing local and national governments, and by raising regular army and local militias Brigadier General Malvar assigned as military commander of Batangas province
30 Jun	First contingent of VIII Corps arrived at Manila
15 Jul	Aguinaldo issued proclamation that all Filipinos were members of the *Katipunan*
26 Jul	Last contingent of VIII Corps arrived in Manila
13 Aug	Battle of Manila: VIII Corps occupied Manila Brigadier General Tinio arrived in Vigan and cleared Ilocos of Spanish forces

	Brigadier General Tinio assigned as military commander of Ilocos region
27 Aug	Major General Otis replaced Major General Merritt as commander of VIII Corps
Sep–Dec	Filipinos held constitutional convention at Malolos
10 Dec	Treaty of Paris signed by United States and Spain

1899

21 Jan	Aguinaldo established government under constitution with Malolos as capital
4/5 Feb	Battle of Manila; Philippine war began
Feb	US Senate ratified Treaty of Paris by one vote
Mar–May	Major General Otis attacked north into central Luzon plain
Mar	Schurman Commission arrived
2 Mar	War Department raised US (federal) volunteer regiments and established 65,000-man Regular Army
31 Mar	Malolos captured
11 Apr	United States and Spain exchange ratified Treaty of Paris; state volunteer regiments eligible for discharge
27 Apr	Calumpit captured
Jun–Nov	Major General Otis reconstituted VIII Corps during summer monsoon and prepared for fall campaign United States Volunteers and Regular regiments arrived
5 Jun	Luna assassinated
Oct–Dec	Major General Otis cleared northern Luzon
12 Nov	Aguinaldo changed *insurrecto* strategy to guerrilla war; dispersed Army of Liberation
23 Nov	Major General MacArthur declared "so-called Filipino republic is destroyed"
Dec	Brigadier General Young occupied Ilocos region

1900

Jan	Brigadier General Tinio reorganized forces in Ilocos for guerrilla warfare

	Major General Otis attacked south of Manila and occupied Tagalog provinces
Jan–Feb	VIII Corps implemented policy of benevolent assimilation by establishing local governments
20 Mar	Brigadier General Tinio issued proclamation promising to punish those who worked with the Americans
29 Mar	VIII Corps reorganized as Division of Philippines with four departments: Ilocos: Major General MacArthur department commander and Brigadier General Young First District Commander; Tagalog region: Major General Bates department commander and Brigadier General Wheaton Second District commander until 16 August when Colonel Birkhimer became acting commander
Mar–Apr	Major General Otis issued general orders on local government and on judicial system
Apr	Father Aglipay's revolt in Ilocos Norte province suppressed
5 May	Major General MacArthur replaced Major General Otis as commander of the Division of the Philippines; Major General Wheaton replaced Major General MacArthur as commander of the Department of Northern Luzon
May	La Union province pacified; Patajo and *Guardia de Honor* worked with Americans; Taft Commission arrived
Jun–Sep	Monsoon season: Lull in Ilocos; increased *insurrecto* activity in Tagalog region
Jun	Brigadier General Young issued general orders targeting supporters of armed *insurrectos*; Major General MacArthur issued amnesty offer; Brigadier General Hall became commander of Second District, Department of Southern Luzon
Jul	Aguinaldo ordered increased attacks in the fall to affect American presidential election
Sep–Oct	Increased *insurrecto* attacks
17 Sep	Brigadier General Cailles defeated American attack at Mabitac in Laguna province

Oct	Brigadier General Malvar reorganized both his guerrilla units and the town support requirements
14 Nov	President McKinley re-elected
2 Dec	First large surrender of 2,180 militiamen at Santa Maria in Ilocos Sur province
Dec	Pro-American Federal Party established in Manila
19–20 Dec	Major General MacArthur declared martial law; began campaign focused on separating the towns from the guerrillas; and issued proclamation to Filipinos explaining their legal status under General Orders 100
21 Dec	Brigadier General Tinio issued proclamation to discourage surrenders

1901

Jan–Apr	Major General MacArthur campaigned to separate the towns from the guerrillas Regulars replaced United States Volunteer regiments Federal Party active in seeking surrender of *insurrectos*
7 Jan	Major General MacArthur deported 26 *insurrecto* leaders to Guam Prisoners of war no longer released; imprisoned for the duration of the insurrection
19 Feb	Brigadier General Young promoted and reassigned
28 Feb	Brigadier General Bell became commander of First District, Department of Northern Luzon
Mar	Lieutenant General Trias surrendered and Aguinaldo captured
Apr	Aguinaldo issued appeal for his followers to accept American rule Brigadier General Malvar issued proclamation assuming command of the *insurrectos* in the Tagalog region General collapse of *insurrecto* movement on Luzon
10 Apr	Brigadier General Hall replaced by Brigadier General Sumner who commanded a consolidated First District that included the Tagalog provinces in Hall's district
27 Apr	Father Aglipay surrendered in Ilocos Norte province

30 Apr	Juan and Blas Villamour surrendered in Abra province
1 May	Brigadier General Tinio surrendered in Ilocos Sur province
	Brigadier General Bell declared First District pacified
May	Major General Bates replaced by Major General Wade as commander of Department of Southern Luzon
24 Jun	Brigadier General Cailles surrendered in Laguna province
4 Jul	Governor Taft replaced Major General MacArthur as governor-general; civil government established
	Major General Chaffee assumed command of the Division of the Philippines
Jul	Brigadier General Malvar assumed command of *insurrectos* and reorganized in the Tagalog provinces
17 Jul	Batangas province and islands of Cebu and Bohol reverted to military government
Sep	Balangiga massacre on Samar
Nov	Division of Philippines reorganized into Department of North Philippines commanded by Major General Wheaton and Department of South Philippines commanded by Major General Wade; each department organized into separate brigades
30 Nov	Brigadier General Bell assumed command of Third Separate Brigade
Dec	Brigadier General Bell prepared for the pacification of Batangas and Laguna provinces: meetings, telegraphic circulars, zones of protection, pressure on towns and on guerrillas

1902

Jan–Apr	Brigadier General Bell conducted systematic campaign to disarm and destroy armed *insurrectos*
10 Jan	Third Separate Brigade's last major contact with *insurrectos*
13 Jan	Third Separate Brigade's first major surrender of *insurrectos*
16 Apr	Brigadier General Malvar surrendered

6 May	Brigadier General Malvar issued proclamation declaring the end of the insurrection
4 Jul	President Roosevelt announced the end of the Philippine Insurrection
	President Roosevelt issued his thanks to the US Army

Appendix B

General Orders 100 [Lieber Code]*

GENERAL ORDERS No. 100.

WAR DEPT., *ADJT. GENERAL'S OFFICE,*

Washington, April 24, 1863.

The following "Instructions for the Government of Armies of the United States in the Field," prepared by Francis Lieber, LL.D., and revised by a board of officers, of which Maj. Gen. E.A. Hitchcock is president, having been approved by the President of the United States, he commands that they be published for the information of all concerned.

By order of the Secretary of War:
E.D. TOWNSEND,
Assistant Adjutant-General.

INSTRUCTIONS FOR THE GOVERNMENT OF ARMIES OF THE UNITED STATES IN THE FIELD.

SECTION I.—*Martial law—Military jurisdiction—Military necessity—Retaliation.*

1.   A place, district, or country occupied by an enemy stands, in consequence of the occupation, under the martial law of the invading or occupying army, whether any proclamation declaring martial law, or any public warning to the inhabitants, has been issued or not. Martial law is the immediate and direct effect and consequence of occupation or conquest.

The presence of a hostile army proclaims its martial law.

2.   Martial law does not cease during the hostile occupation, except by special proclamation, ordered by the commander-in-chief, or by special mention in the treaty of peace concluding the war, when the occupation of a place or territory continues beyond the conclusion of peace as one of the conditions of the same.

---

*War Department, "General Orders No. 100, Instructions for the Government of Armies of the United States in the Field, 24 April 1863." Document online, available at <http://www.usregulars.com/Lieber.html>, accessed 30 May 2007. Specific articles emphasized by Brigadier General J. Franklin Bell in his 1901–02 *Telegraphic Circulars* to his subordinates in southwestern Luzon are highlighted in **BOLD** print.

3. Martial law in a hostile country consists in the suspension by the occupying military authority of the criminal and civil law, and of the domestic administration and government in the occupied place or territory, and in the substitution of military rule and force for the same, as well as in the dictation of general laws, as far as military necessity requires this suspension, substitution, or dictation.

The commander of the forces may proclaim that the administration of all civil and penal law shall continue either wholly or in part, as in times of peace, unless otherwise ordered by the military authority.

4. Martial law is simply military authority exercised in accordance with the laws and usages of war. Military oppression is not martial law; it is the abuse of the power which that law confers. As martial law is executed by military force, it is incumbent upon those who administer it to be strictly guided by the principles of justice, honor, and humanity—virtues adorning a soldier even more than other men, for the very reason that he possesses the power of his arms against the unarmed.

5. Martial law should be less stringent in places and countries fully occupied and fairly conquered. Much greater severity may be exercised in places or regions where actual hostilities exist or are expected and must be prepared for. Its most complete sway is allowed—even in the commander's own country—when face to face with the enemy, because of the absolute necessities of the case, and of the paramount duty to defend the country against invasion.

To save the country is paramount to all other considerations.

6. All civil and penal law shall continue to take its usual course in the enemy's places and territories under martial law, unless interrupted or stopped by order of the occupying military power; but all the functions of the hostile government—legislative, executive, or administrative—whether of a general, provincial, or local character, cease under martial law, or continue only with the sanction, or, if deemed necessary, the participation of the occupier or invader.

7. Martial law extends to property, and to persons, whether they are subjects of the enemy or aliens to that government.

8. Consuls, among American and European nations, are not diplomatic agents. Nevertheless, their offices and persons will be subjected to martial law in cases of urgent necessity only; their property and business are not exempted. Any delinquency they commit against the established military rule may be punished as in the case of any other inhabitant, and such punishment furnishes no reasonable ground for international complaint.

9. The functions of ambassadors, ministers, or other diplomatic agents, accredited by neutral powers to the hostile government, cease, so far as regards the displaced government; but the conquering or occupying power usually recognizes them as temporarily accredited to itself.

10. Martial law affects chiefly the police and collection of public revenue and taxes, whether imposed by the expelled government or by the invader, and refers mainly to the support and efficiency of the Army, its safety, and the safety of its operations.

11. The law of war does not only disclaim all cruelty and bad faith concerning engagements concluded with the enemy during the war, but also the breaking of stipulations solemnly contracted by the belligerents in time of peace, and avowedly intended to remain in force in case of war between the contracting powers.

It disclaims all extortions and other transactions for individual gain; all acts of private revenge, or connivance at such acts.

Offenses to the contrary shall be severely punished, and especially so if committed by officers.

12. Whenever feasible, martial law is carried out in cases of individual offenders by military courts; but sentences of death shall be executed only with the approval of the chief executive, provided the urgency of the case does not require a speedier execution, and then only with the approval of the chief commander.

13. Military jurisdiction is of two kinds: First, that which is conferred and defined by statute; second, that which is derived from the common law of war. Military offenses under the statute law must be tried in the manner therein directed; but military offenses which do not come within the statute must be tried and punished under the common law of war. The character of the courts which exercise these jurisdictions depends upon the local laws of each particular country.

In the armies of the United States the first is exercised by courts-martial; while cases which do not come within the Rules and Articles of War, or the jurisdiction conferred by statute on courts-martial, are tried by military commissions.

14. Military necessity, as understood by modern civilized nations, consists in the necessity of those measures which are indispensable for securing the ends of the war, and which are lawful according to the modern law and usages of war.

15. Military necessity admits of all direct destruction of life or limb of armed enemies, and of other persons whose destruction is incidentally

unavoidable in the armed contests of the war; it allows of the capturing of every armed enemy, and every enemy of importance to the hostile government, or of peculiar danger to the captor; it allows of all destruction of property, and obstruction of the ways and channels of traffic, travel, or communication, and of all withholding of sustenance or means of life from the enemy; of the appropriation of whatever an enemy's country affords necessary for the subsistence and safety of the Army, and of such deception as does not involve the breaking of good faith either positively pledged, regarding agreements entered into during the war, or supposed by the modern law of war to exist. Men who take up arms against one another in public war do not cease on this account to be moral beings, responsible to one another and to God.

16. Military necessity does not admit of cruelty—that is, the infliction of suffering for the sake of suffering or for revenge, nor of maiming or wounding except in fight, nor of torture to extort confessions. It does not admit of the use of poison in any way, nor of the wanton devastation of a district. It admits of deception, but disclaims acts of perfidy; and, in general, military necessity does not include any act of hostility which makes the return to peace unnecessarily difficult.

17. War is not carried on by arms alone. It is lawful to starve the hostile belligerent, armed or unarmed, so that it leads to the speedier subjection of the enemy.

18. When a commander of a besieged place expels the non-combatants, in order to lessen the number of those who consume his stock of provisions, it is lawful, though an extreme measure, to drive them back, so as to hasten on the surrender.

19. Commanders, whenever admissible, inform the enemy of their intention to bombard a place, so that the non-combatants, and especially the women and children, may be removed before the bombardment commences. But it is no infraction of the common law of war to omit thus to inform the enemy. Surprise may be a necessity.

20. Public war is a state of armed hostility between sovereign nations or governments. It is a law and requisite of civilized existence that men live in political, continuous societies, forming organized units, called states or nations, whose constituents bear, enjoy, and suffer, advance and retrograde together, in peace and in war.

21. The citizen or native of a hostile country is thus an enemy, as one of the constituents of the hostile state or nation, and as such is subjected to the hardships of the war.

22. Nevertheless, as civilization has advanced during the last centuries, so has likewise steadily advanced, especially in war on land, the distinction between the private individual belonging to a hostile country and the hostile country itself, with its men in arms. The principle has been more and more acknowledged that the unarmed citizen is to be spared in person, property, and honor as much as the exigencies of war will admit.

23. Private citizens are no longer murdered, enslaved, or carried off to distant parts, and the inoffensive individual is as little disturbed in his private relations as the commander of the hostile troops can afford to grant in the overruling demands of a vigorous war.

24. The almost universal rule in remote times was, and continues to be with barbarous armies, that the private individual of the hostile country is destined to suffer every privation of liberty and protection and every disruption of family ties. Protection was, and still is with uncivilized people, the exception.

25. In modern regular wars of the Europeans and their descendants in other portions of the globe, protection of the inoffensive citizen of the hostile country is the rule; privation and disturbance of private relations are the exceptions.

26. Commanding generals may cause the magistrates and civil officers of the hostile country to take the oath of temporary allegiance or an oath of fidelity to their own victorious government or rulers, and they may expel every one who declines to do so. But whether they do so or not, the people and their civil officers owe strict obedience to them as long as they hold sway over the district or country, at the peril of their lives.

27. The law of war can no more wholly dispense with retaliation than can the law of nations, of which it is a branch. Yet civilized nations acknowledge retaliation as the sternest feature of war. A reckless enemy often leaves to his opponent no other means of securing himself against the repetition of barbarous outrage.

28. Retaliation will therefore never be resorted to as a measure of mere revenge, but only as a means of protective retribution, and moreover cautiously and unavoidably—that is to say, retaliation shall only be resorted to after careful inquiry into the real occurrence and the character of the misdeeds that may demand retribution.

Unjust or inconsiderate retaliation removes the belligerents farther and farther from the mitigating rules of regular war, and by rapid steps leads them nearer to the internecine wars of savages.

29. Modern times are distinguished from earlier ages by the existence at one and the same time of many nations and great governments related to one another in close intercourse.

Peace is their normal condition; war is the exception. The ultimate object of all modern war is a renewed state of peace.

The more vigorously wars are pursued the better it is for humanity. Sharp wars are brief.

30. Ever since the formation and coexistence of modern nations, and ever since wars have become great national wars, war has come to be acknowledged not to be its own end, but the means to obtain great ends of state, or to consist in defense against wrong; and no conventional restriction of the modes adopted to injure the enemy is any longer admitted; but the law of war imposes many limitations and restrictions on principles of justice, faith, and honor.

SECTION II.—*Public and private property of the enemy—Protection of persons, and especially of women; of religion, the arts and sciences— Punishment of crimes against the inhabitants of hostile countries.*

31. A victorious army appropriates all public money, seizes all public movable property until further direction by its government, and sequesters for its own benefit or of that of its government all the revenues of real property belonging to the hostile government or nation. The title to such real property remains in abeyance during military occupation, and until the conquest is made complete.

32. A victorious army, by the martial power inherent in the same, may suspend, change, or abolish, as far as the martial power extends, the relations which arise from the services due, according to the existing laws of the invaded country, from one citizen, subject, or native of the same to another.

The commander of the army must leave it to the ultimate treaty of peace to settle the permanency of this change.

33. It is no longer considered lawful—on the contrary, it is held to be a serious breach of the law of war—to force the subjects of the enemy into the service of the victorious government, except the latter should proclaim, after a fair and complete conquest of the hostile country or district, that it is resolved to keep the country, district, or place permanently as its own and make it a portion of its own country.

34. As a general rule, the property belonging to churches, to hospitals, or other establishments of an exclusively charitable character,

to establishments of education, or foundations for the promotion of knowledge, whether public schools, universities, academies of learning or observatories, museums of the fine arts, or of a scientific character—such property is not to be considered public property in the sense of paragraph 31; but it may be taxed or used when the public service may require it.

35. Classical works of art, libraries, scientific collections, or precious instruments, such as astronomical telescopes, as well as hospitals, must be secured against all avoidable injury, even when they are contained in fortified places whilst besieged or bombarded.

36. If such works of art, libraries, collections, or instruments belonging to a hostile nation or government, can be removed without injury, the ruler of the conquering state or nation may order them to be seized and removed for the benefit of the said nation. The ultimate ownership is to be settled by the ensuing treaty of peace.

In no case shall they be sold or given away, if captured by the armies of the United States, nor shall they ever be privately appropriated, or wantonly destroyed or injured.

37. The United States acknowledge and protect, in hostile countries occupied by them, religion and morality; strictly private property; the persons of the inhabitants, especially those of women; and the sacredness of domestic relations. Offenses to the contrary shall be rigorously punished.

This rule does not interfere with the right of the victorious invader to tax the people or their property, to levy forced loans, to billet soldiers, or to appropriate property, especially houses, lands, boats or ships, and the churches, for temporary and military uses.

38. Private property, unless forfeited by crimes or by offenses of the owner, can be seized only by way of military necessity, for the support or other benefit of the Army or of the United States.

If the owner has not fled, the commanding officer will cause receipts to be given, which may serve the spoliated owner to obtain indemnity.

39. The salaries of civil officers of the hostile government who remain in the invaded territory, and continue the work of their office, and can continue it according to the circumstances arising out of the war—such as judges, administrative or political officers, officers of city or communal governments—are paid from the public revenue of the invaded territory until the military government has reason wholly or partially to discontinue

it. Salaries or incomes connected with purely honorary titles are always stopped.

40. There exists no law or body of authoritative rules of action between hostile armies, except that branch of the law of nature and nations which is called the law and usages of war on land.

41. All municipal law of the ground on which the armies stand, or of the countries to which they belong, is silent and of no effect between armies in the field.

42. Slavery, complicating and confounding the ideas of property (that is, of a thing), and of personality (that is, of humanity), exists according to municipal or local law only. The law of nature and nations has never acknowledged it. The digest of the Roman law enacts the early dictum of the pagan jurist, that "so far as the law of nature is concerned, all men are equal." Fugitives escaping from a country in which they were slaves, villains, or serfs, into another country, have, for centuries past, been held free and acknowledged free by judicial decisions of European countries, even though the municipal law of the country in which the slave had taken refuge acknowledged slavery within its own dominions.

43. Therefore, in a war between the United States and a belligerent which admits of slavery, if a person held in bondage by that belligerent be captured by or come as a fugitive under the protection of the military forces of the United States, such person is immediately entitled to the rights and privileges of a freeman. To return such person into slavery would amount to enslaving a free person, and neither the United States nor any officer under their authority can enslave any human being. Moreover, a person so made free by the law of war is under the shield of the law of nations, and the former owner or State can have, by the law of postliminy, no belligerent lien or claim of service.

44. All wanton violence committed against persons in the invaded country, all destruction of property not commanded by the authorized officer, all robbery, all pillage or sacking, even after taking a place by main force, all rape, wounding, maiming, or killing of such inhabitants, are prohibited under the penalty of death, or such other severe punishment as may seem adequate for the gravity of the offense.

A soldier, officer, or private, in the act of committing such violence, and disobeying a superior ordering him to abstain from it, may be lawfully killed on the spot by such superior.

45. All captures and booty belong, according to the modern law of war, primarily to the government of the captor.

Prize money, whether on sea or land, can now only be claimed under local law.

46. Neither officers nor soldiers are allowed to make use of their position or power in the hostile country for private gain, not even for commercial transactions otherwise legitimate. Offenses to the contrary committed by commissioned officers will be punished with cashiering or such other punishment as the nature of the offense may require; if by soldiers, they shall be punished according to the nature of the offense.

47. Crimes punishable by all penal codes, such as arson, murder, maiming, assaults, highway robbery, theft, burglary, fraud, forgery, and rape, if committed by an American soldier in a hostile country against its inhabitants, are not only punishable as at home, but in all cases in which death is not inflicted the severer punishment shall be preferred.

SECTION III.—*Deserters—Prisoners of war—Hostages—Booty on the battle-field.*

48. Deserters from the American Army, having entered the service of the enemy, suffer death if they fall again into the hands of the United States, whether by capture or being delivered up to the American Army; and if a deserter from the enemy, having taken service in the Army of the United States, is captured by the enemy, and punished by them with death or otherwise, it is not a breach against the law and usages of war, requiring redress or retaliation.

49. A prisoner of war is a public enemy armed or attached to the hostile army for active aid, who has fallen into the hands of the captor, either fighting or wounded, on the field or in the hospital, by individual surrender or by capitulation.

All soldiers, of whatever species of arms; all men who belong to the rising *en masse* of the hostile country; all those who are attached to the Army for its efficiency and promote directly the object of the war, except such as are hereinafter provided for; all disabled men or officers on the field or elsewhere, if captured; all enemies who have thrown away their arms and ask for quarter, are prisoners of war, and as such exposed to the inconveniences as well as entitled to the privileges of a prisoner of war.

50. Moreover, citizens who accompany an army for whatever purpose, such as sutlers, editors, or reporters of journals, or contractors, if captured, may be made prisoners of war and be detained as such.

The monarch and members of the hostile reigning family, male or female, the chief, and chief officers of the hostile government, its diplomatic agents, and all persons who are of particular and singular use and benefit to the hostile army or its government, are, if captured on belligerent ground, and if unprovided with a safe-conduct granted by the captor's government, prisoners of war.

51. If the people of that portion of an invaded country which is not yet occupied by the enemy, or of the whole country, at the approach of a hostile army, rise, under a duly authorized levy, *en masse* to resist the invader, they are now treated as public enemies, and, if captured, are prisoners of war.

52. No belligerent has the right to declare that he will treat every captured man in arms of a levy *en masse* as a brigand or bandit.

If, however, the people of a country, or any portion of the same, already occupied by an army, rise against it, they are violators of the laws of war and are not entitled to their protection.

53. The enemy's chaplains, officers of the medical staff, apothecaries, hospital nurses, and servants, if they fall into the hands of the American Army, are not prisoners of war, unless the commander has reasons to retain them. In this latter case, or if, at their own desire, they are allowed to remain with their captured companions, they are treated as prisoners of war, and may be exchanged if the commander sees fit.

54. A hostage is a person accepted as a pledge for the fulfillment of an agreement concluded between belligerents during the war, or in consequence of a war. Hostages are rare in the present age.

55. If a hostage is accepted, he is treated like a prisoner of war, according to rank and condition, as circumstances may admit.

56. A prisoner of war is subject to no punishment for being a public enemy, nor is any revenge wreaked upon him by the intentional infliction of any suffering, or disgrace, by cruel imprisonment, want of food, by mutilation, death, or any other barbarity.

57. So soon as a man is armed by a sovereign government and takes the soldier's oath of fidelity he is a belligerent; his killing, wounding, or other warlike acts are no individual crimes or offenses. No belligerent has a right to declare that enemies of a certain class, color, or condition, when properly organized as soldiers, will not be treated by him as public enemies.

58. The law of nations knows of no distinction of color, and if an enemy of the United States should enslave and sell any captured persons of

their Army, it would be a case for the severest retaliation, if not redressed upon complaint.

The United States cannot retaliate by enslavement; therefore death must be the retaliation for this crime against the law of nations.

59. A prisoner of war remains answerable for his crimes committed against the captor's army or people, committed before he was captured, and for which he has not been punished by his own authorities.

All prisoners of war are liable to the infliction of retaliatory measures.

60. It is against the usage of modern war to resolve, in hatred and revenge, to give no quarter. No body of troops has the right to declare that it will not give, and therefore will not expect, quarter; but a commander is permitted to direct his troops to give no quarter, in great straits, when his own salvation makes it impossible to cumber himself with prisoners.

61. Troops that give no quarter have no right to kill enemies already disabled on the ground, or prisoners captured by other troops.

62. All troops of the enemy known or discovered to give no quarter in general, or to any portion of the Army, receive none.

63. Troops who fight in the uniform of their enemies, without any plain, striking, and uniform mark of distinction of their own, can expect no quarter.

64. If American troops capture a train containing uniforms of the enemy, and the commander considers it advisable to distribute them for use among his men, some striking mark or sign must be adopted to distinguish the American soldier from the enemy.

65. The use of the enemy's national standard, flag, or other emblem of nationality, for the purpose of deceiving the enemy in battle, is an act of perfidy by which they lose all claim to the protection of the laws of war.

66. Quarter having been given to an enemy by American troops, under a misapprehension of his true character, he may, nevertheless, be ordered to suffer death if, within three days after the battle, it be discovered that he belongs to a corps which gives no quarter.

67. The law of nations allows every sovereign government to make war upon another sovereign State, and, therefore, admits of no rules or laws different from those of regular warfare, regarding the treatment of

prisoners of war, although they may belong to the army of a government which the captor may consider as a wanton and unjust assailant.

68. Modern wars are not internecine wars, in which the killing of the enemy is the object. The destruction of the enemy in modern war, and, indeed, modern war itself, are means to obtain that object of the belligerent which lies beyond the war.

Unnecessary or revengeful destruction of life is not lawful.

69. Outposts, sentinels, or pickets are not to be fired upon, except to drive them in, or when a positive order, special or general, has been issued to that effect.

70. The use of poison in any manner, be it to poison wells, or food, or arms, is wholly excluded from modern warfare. He that uses it puts himself out of the pale of the law and usages of war.

71. Whoever intentionally inflicts additional wounds on an enemy already wholly disabled, or kills such an enemy, or who orders or encourages soldiers to do so, shall suffer death, if duly convicted, whether he belongs to the Army of the United States, or is an enemy captured after having committed his misdeed.

72. Money and other valuables on the person of a prisoner, such as watches or jewelry, as well as extra clothing, are regarded by the American Army as the private property of the prisoner, and the appropriation of such valuables or money is considered dishonorable, and is prohibited.

Nevertheless, if large sums are found upon the persons of prisoners, or in their possession, they shall be taken from them, and the surplus, after providing for their own support, appropriated for the use of the Army, under the direction of the commander, unless otherwise ordered by the Government. Nor can prisoners claim, as private property, large sums found and captured in their train, although they have been placed in the private luggage of the prisoners.

73. All officers, when captured, must surrender their side-arms to the captor. They may be restored to the prisoner in marked cases, by the commander, to signalize admiration of his distinguished bravery, or approbation of his humane treatment of prisoners before his capture. The captured officer to whom they may be restored cannot wear them during captivity.

74. A prisoner of war, being a public enemy, is the prisoner of the Government and not of the captor. No ransom can be paid by a prisoner of war to his individual captor, or to any officer in command. The Government alone releases captives, according to rules prescribed by itself.

75. Prisoners of war are subject to confinement or imprisonment such as may be deemed necessary on account of safety, but they are to be subjected to no other intentional suffering or indignity. The confinement and mode of treating a prisoner may be varied during his captivity according to the demands of safety.

76. Prisoners of war shall be fed upon plain and wholesome food, whenever practicable, and treated with humanity.

They may be required to work for the benefit of the captor's government, according to their rank and condition.

77. A prisoner of war who escapes may be shot, or otherwise killed, in his flight; but neither death nor any other punishment shall be inflicted upon him simply for his attempt to escape, which the law of war does not consider a crime. Stricter means of security shall be used after an unsuccessful attempt at escape.

If, however, a conspiracy is discovered, the purpose of which is a united or general escape, the conspirators may be rigorously punished, even with death; and capital punishment may also be inflicted upon prisoners of war discovered to have plotted rebellion against the authorities of the captors, whether in union with fellow-prisoners or other persons.

78. If prisoners of war, having given no pledge nor made any promise on their honor, forcibly or otherwise escape, and are captured again in battle, after having rejoined their own army, they shall not be punished for their escape, but shall be treated as simple prisoners of war, although they will be subjected to stricter confinement.

79. Every captured wounded enemy shall be medically treated, according to the ability of the medical staff.

80. Honorable men, when captured, will abstain from giving to the enemy information concerning their own army, and the modern law of war permits no longer the use of any violence against prisoners in order to extort the desired information, or to punish them for having given false information.

SECTION IV.—*Partisans—Armed enemies not belonging to the hostile army—Scouts—Armed prowlers—War-rebels.*

81. Partisans are soldiers armed and wearing the uniform of their army, but belonging to a corps which acts detached from the main body for the purpose of making inroads into the territory occupied by the enemy. If captured they are entitled to all the privileges of the prisoner of war.

82. Men, or squads of men, who commit hostilities, whether by fighting, or inroads for destruction or plunder, or by raids of any kind, without commission, without being part and portion of the organized hostile army, and without sharing continuously in the war, but who do so with intermitting returns to their homes and avocations, or with the occasional assumption of the semblance of peaceful pursuits, divesting themselves of the character or appearance of soldiers—such men, or squads of men, are not public enemies, and therefore, if captured, are not entitled to the privileges of prisoners of war, but shall be treated summarily as highway robbers or pirates.

83. Scouts or single soldiers, if disguised in the dress of the country, or in the uniform of the army hostile to their own, employed in obtaining information, if found within or lurking about the lines of the captor, are treated as spies, and suffer death.

84. Armed prowlers, by whatever names they may be called, or persons of the enemy's territory, who steal within the lines of the hostile army for the purpose of robbing, killing, or of destroying bridges, roads, or canals, or of robbing or destroying the mail, or of cutting the telegraph wires, are not entitled to the privileges of the prisoner of war.

85. War-rebels are persons within an occupied territory who rise in arms against the occupying or conquering army, or against the authorities established by the same. If captured, they may suffer death, whether they rise singly, in small or large bands, and whether called upon to do so by their own, but expelled, government or not. They are not prisoners of war; nor are they if discovered and secured before their conspiracy has matured to an actual rising or to armed violence.

SECTION V.—*Safe-conduct—Spies—War-traitors—Captured messengers—Abuse of the flag of truce.*

86. All intercourse between the territories occupied by belligerent armies, whether by traffic, by letter, by travel, or in any other way, ceases. This is the general rule, to be observed without special proclamation.

Exceptions to this rule, whether by safe-conduct or permission to trade on a small or large scale, or by exchanging mails, or by travel from one territory into the other, can take place only according to agreement approved by the Government or by the highest military authority.

Contraventions of this rule are highly punishable.

87. Ambassadors, and all other diplomatic agents of neutral powers accredited to the enemy may receive safe-conducts through the territories occupied by the belligerents, unless there are military reasons to the contrary, and unless they may reach the place of their destination conveniently by another route. It implies no international affront if the safe-conduct is declined. Such passes are usually given by the supreme authority of the state and not by subordinate officers.

88. A spy is a person who secretly, in disguise or under false pretense, seeks information with the intention of communicating it to the enemy.

The spy is punishable with death by hanging by the neck, whether or not he succeed in obtaining the information or in conveying it to the enemy.

89. If a citizen of the United States obtains information in a legitimate manner and betrays it to the enemy, be he a military or civil officer, or a private citizen, he shall suffer death.

90. A traitor under the law of war, or a war-traitor, is a person in a place or district under martial law who, unauthorized by the military commander, gives information of any kind to the enemy, or holds intercourse with him.

91. The war-traitor is always severely punished. If his offense consists in betraying to the enemy anything concerning the condition, safety, operations, or plans of the troops holding or occupying the place or district, his punishment is death.

92. If the citizen or subject of a country or place invaded or conquered gives information to his own government, from which he is separated by the hostile army, or to the army of his government, he is a war-traitor, and death is the penalty of his offense.

93. All armies in the field stand in need of guides, and impress them if they cannot obtain them otherwise.

94. No person having been forced by the enemy to serve as guide is punishable for having done so.

95. If a citizen of a hostile and invaded district voluntarily serves as a guide to the enemy, or offers to do so, he is deemed a war-traitor and shall suffer death.

96. A citizen serving voluntarily as a guide against his own country commits treason, and will be dealt with according to the law of his country.

97. Guides, when it is clearly proved that they have misled intentionally, may be put to death.

98. All unauthorized or secret communication with the enemy is considered treasonable by the law of war.

Foreign residents in an invaded or occupied territory or foreign visitors in the same can claim no immunity from this law. They may communicate with foreign parts or with the inhabitants of the hostile country, so far as the military authority permits, but no further. Instant expulsion from the occupied territory would be the very least punishment for the infraction of this rule.

99. A messenger carrying written dispatches or verbal messages from one portion of the army or from a besieged place to another portion of the same army or its government, if armed, and in the uniform of his army, and if captured while doing so in the territory occupied by the enemy, is treated by the captor as a prisoner of war. If not in uniform nor a soldier, the circumstances connected with his capture must determine the disposition that shall be made of him.

100. A messenger or agent who attempts to steal through the territory occupied by the enemy to further in any manner the interests of the enemy, if captured, is not entitled to the privileges of the prisoner of war, and may be dealt with according to the circumstances of the case.

101. While deception in war is admitted as a just and necessary means of hostility, and is consistent with honorable warfare, the common law of war allows even capital punishment for clandestine or treacherous attempts to injure an enemy, because they are so dangerous, and it is so difficult to guard against them.

102. The law of war, like the criminal law regarding other offenses, makes no difference on account of the difference of sexes, concerning the spy, the war-traitor, or the war-rebel.

103. Spies, war-traitors, and war-rebels are not exchanged according to the common law of war. The exchange of such persons would require a special cartel, authorized by the Government, or, at a great distance from it, by the chief commander of the army in the field.

104. A successful spy or war-traitor, safely returned to his own army, and afterward captured as an enemy, is not subject to punishment for his acts as a spy or war-traitor, but he may be held in closer custody as a person individually dangerous.

SECTION VI.—*Exchange of prisoners—Flags of truce—Flags of protection.*

105. Exchanges of prisoners take place—number for number—rank for rank—wounded for wounded—with added condition for added condition—such, for instance, as not to serve for a certain period.

106. In exchanging prisoners of war, such numbers of persons of inferior rank may be substituted as an equivalent for one of superior rank as may be agreed upon by cartel, which requires the sanction of the Government, or of the commander of the army in the field.

107. A prisoner of war is in honor bound truly to state to the captor his rank; and he is not to assume a lower rank than belongs to him, in order to cause a more advantageous exchange, nor a higher rank, for the purpose of obtaining better treatment.

Offenses to the contrary have been justly punished by the commanders of released prisoners, and may be good cause for refusing to release such prisoners.

108. The surplus number of prisoners of war remaining after an exchange has taken place is sometimes released either for the payment of a stipulated sum of money, or, in urgent cases, of provision, clothing, or other necessaries.

Such arrangement, however, requires the sanction of the highest authority.

109. The exchange of prisoners of war is an act of convenience to both belligerents. If no general cartel has been concluded, it cannot be demanded by either of them. No belligerent is obliged to exchange prisoners of war.

A cartel is voidable as soon as either party has violated it.

110. No exchange of prisoners shall be made except after complete capture, and after an accurate account of them, and a list of the captured officers, has been taken.

111. The bearer of a flag of truce cannot insist upon being admitted. He must always be admitted with great caution. Unnecessary frequency is carefully to be avoided.

112. If the bearer of a flag of truce offer himself during an engagement, he can be admitted as a very rare exception only. It is no breach of good faith to retain such flag of truce, if admitted during the engagement. Firing is not required to cease on the appearance of a flag of truce in battle.

113. If the bearer of a flag of truce, presenting himself during an engagement, is killed or wounded, it furnishes no ground of complaint whatever.

114. If it be discovered, and fairly proved, that a flag of truce has been abused for surreptitiously obtaining military knowledge, the bearer of the flag thus abusing his sacred character is deemed a spy.

So sacred is the character of a flag of truce, and so necessary is its sacredness, that while its abuse is an especially heinous offense, great caution is requisite, on the other hand, in convicting the bearer of a flag of truce as a spy.

115. It is customary to designate by certain flags (usually yellow) the hospitals in places which are shelled, so that the besieging enemy may avoid firing on them. The same has been done in battles when hospitals are situated within the field of the engagement.

116. Honorable belligerents often request that the hospitals within the territory of the enemy may be designated, so that they may be spared.

An honorable belligerent allows himself to be guided by flags or signals of protection as much as the contingencies and the necessities of the fight will permit.

117. It is justly considered an act of bad faith, of infamy or fiendishness, to deceive the enemy by flags of protection. Such act of bad faith may be good cause for refusing to respect such flags.

118. The besieging belligerent has sometimes requested the besieged to designate the buildings containing collections of works of art, scientific museums, astronomical observatories, or precious libraries, so that their destruction may be avoided as much as possible.

SECTION VII.—*The parole.*

119. Prisoners of war may be released from captivity by exchange, and, under certain circumstances, also by parole.

120. The term parole designates the pledge of individual good faith and honor to do, or to omit doing, certain acts after he who gives his parole shall have been dismissed, wholly or partially, from the power of the captor.

121. The pledge of the parole is always an individual, but not a private act.

122. The parole applies chiefly to prisoners of war whom the captor allows to return to their country, or to live in greater freedom within the captor's country or territory, on conditions stated in the parole.

123. Release of prisoners of war by exchange is the general rule; release by parole is the exception.

124. Breaking the parole is punished with death when the person breaking the parole is captured again.

Accurate lists, therefore, of the paroled persons must be kept by the belligerents.

125. When paroles are given and received there must be an exchange of two written documents, in which the name and rank of the paroled individuals are accurately and truthfully stated.

126. Commissioned officers only are allowed to give their parole, and they can give it only with the permission of their superior, as long as a superior in rank is within reach.

127. No non-commissioned officer or private can give his parole except through an officer. Individual paroles not given through an officer are not only void, but subject the individuals giving them to the punishment of death as deserters. The only admissible exception is where individuals, properly separated from their commands, have suffered long confinement without the possibility of being paroled through an officer.

128. No paroling on the battle-field; no paroling of entire bodies of troops after a battle; and no dismissal of large numbers of prisoners, with a general declaration that they are paroled, is permitted, or of any value.

129. In capitulations for the surrender of strong places or fortified camps the commanding officer, in cases of urgent necessity, may agree that the troops under his command shall not fight again during the war unless exchanged.

130. The usual pledge given in the parole is not to serve during the existing war unless exchanged.

This pledge refers only to the active service in the field against the paroling belligerent or his allies actively engaged in the same war. These cases of breaking the parole are patent acts, and can be visited with the punishment of death; but the pledge does not refer to internal service, such as recruiting or drilling the recruits, fortifying places not besieged, quelling civil commotions, fighting against belligerents unconnected with the paroling belligerents, or to civil or diplomatic service for which the paroled officer may be employed.

131. If the government does not approve of the parole, the paroled officer must return into captivity, and should the enemy refuse to receive him he is free of his parole.

132. A belligerent government may declare, by a general order, whether it will allow paroling and on what conditions it will allow it. Such order is communicated to the enemy.

133. No prisoner of war can be forced by the hostile government to parole himself, and no government is obliged to parole prisoners of war or to parole all captured officers, if it paroles any. As the pledging of the parole is an individual act, so is paroling, on the other hand, an act of choice on the part of the belligerent.

134. The commander of an occupying army may require of the civil officers of the enemy, and of its citizens, any pledge he may consider necessary for the safety or security of his army, and upon their failure to give it he may arrest, confine, or detain them.

SECTION VIII.—*Armistice—Capitulation.*

135. An armistice is the cessation of active hostilities for a period agreed between belligerents. It must be agreed upon in writing and duly ratified by the highest authorities of the contending parties.

136. If an armistice be declared without conditions it extends no further than to require a total cessation of hostilities along the front of both belligerents.

If conditions be agreed upon, they should be clearly expressed, and must be rigidly adhered to by both parties. If either party violates any express condition, the armistice may be declared null and void by the other.

137. An armistice may be general, and valid for all points and lines of the belligerents; or special—that is, referring to certain troops or certain localities only. An armistice may be concluded for a definite time; or for an indefinite time, during which either belligerent may resume hostilities on giving the notice agreed upon to the other.

138. The motives which induce the one or the other belligerent to conclude an armistice, whether it be expected to be preliminary to a treaty of peace, or to prepare during the armistice for a more vigorous prosecution of the war, does in no way affect the character of the armistice itself.

139. An armistice is binding upon the belligerents from the day of the agreed commencement; but the officers of the armies are responsible from the day only when they receive official information of its existence.

140. Commanding officers have the right to conclude armistices binding on the district over which their command extends, but such armistice is subject to the ratification of the superior authority, and ceases so soon

154

as it is made known to the enemy that the armistice is not ratified, even if a certain time for the elapsing between giving notice of cessation and the resumption of hostilities should have been stipulated for.

141. It is incumbent upon the contracting parties of an armistice to stipulate what intercourse of persons or traffic between the inhabitants of the territories occupied by the hostile armies shall be allowed, if any.

If nothing is stipulated the intercourse remains suspended, as during actual hostilities.

142. An armistice is not a partial or a temporary peace; it is only the suspension of military operations to the extent agreed upon by the parties.

143. When an armistice is concluded between a fortified place and the army besieging it, it is agreed by all the authorities on this subject that the besieger must cease all extension, perfection, or advance of his attacking works as much so as from attacks by main force.

But as there is a difference of opinion among martial jurists whether the besieged have a right to repair breaches or to erect new works of defense within the place during an armistice, this point should be determined by express agreement between the parties.

144. So soon as a capitulation is signed the capitulator has no right to demolish, destroy, or injure the works, arms, stores, or ammunition in his possession, during the time which elapses between the signing and the execution of the capitulation, unless otherwise stipulated in the same.

145. When an armistice is clearly broken by one of the parties the other party is released from all obligation to observe it.

146. Prisoners taken in the act of breaking an armistice must be treated as prisoners of war, the officer alone being responsible who gives the order for such a violation of an armistice. The highest authority of the belligerent aggrieved may demand redress for the infraction of an armistice.

147. Belligerents sometimes conclude an armistice while their plenipotentiaries are met to discuss the conditions of a treaty of peace; but plenipotentiaries may meet without a preliminary armistice; in the latter case the war is carried on without any abatement.

SECTION IX.—*Assassination.*

148. The law of war does not allow proclaiming either an individual belonging to the hostile army, or a citizen, or a subject of the hostile government an outlaw, who may be slain without trial by any

captor, any more than the modern law of peace allows such international outlawry; on the contrary, it abhors such outrage. The sternest retaliation should follow the murder committed in consequence of such proclamation, made by whatever authority. Civilized nations look with horror upon offers of rewards for the assassination of enemies as relapses into barbarism.

SECTION X.—*Insurrection—Civil war—Rebellion.*

149. Insurrection is the rising of people in arms against their government, or portion of it, or against one or more of its laws, or against an officer or officers of the government. It may be confined to mere armed resistance, or it may have greater ends in view.

150. Civil war is war between two or more portions of a country or state, each contending for the mastery of the whole, and each claiming to be the legitimate government. The term is also sometimes applied to war of rebellion, when the rebellious provinces or portions of the state are contiguous to those containing the seat of government.

151. The term rebellion is applied to an insurrection of large extent, and is usually a war between the legitimate government of a country and portions of provinces of the same who seek to throw off their allegiance to it and set up a government of their own.

152. When humanity induces the adoption of the rules of regular war toward rebels, whether the adoption is partial or entire, it does in no way whatever imply a partial or complete acknowledgment of their government, if they have set up one, or of them, as an independent or sovereign power. Neutrals have no right to make the adoption of the rules of war by the assailed government toward rebels the ground of their own acknowledgment of the revolted people as an independent power.

153. Treating captured rebels as prisoners of war, exchanging them, concluding of cartels, capitulations, or other warlike agreements with them; addressing officers of a rebel army by the rank they may have in the same; accepting flags of truce; or, on the other hand, proclaiming martial law in their territory, or levying war taxes or forced loans, or doing any other act sanctioned or demanded by the law and usages of public war between sovereign belligerents, neither proves nor establishes an acknowledgment of the rebellious people, or of the government which they may have erected, as a public or sovereign power. Nor does the adoption of the rules of war toward rebels imply an engagement with them extending beyond the limits of these rules. It is victory in the field that ends the strife and settles the future relations between the contending parties.

154. Treating in the field the rebellious enemy according to the law and usages of war has never prevented the legitimate government from trying the leaders of the rebellion or chief rebels for high treason, and from treating them accordingly, unless they are included in a general amnesty.

155. All enemies in regular war are divided into two general classes—that is to say, into combatants and non-combatants, or unarmed citizens of the hostile government.

The military commander of the legitimate government, in a war of rebellion, distinguishes between the loyal citizen in the revolted portion of the country and the disloyal citizen. The disloyal citizens may further be classified into those citizens known to sympathize with the rebellion without positively aiding it, and those who, without taking up arms, give positive aid and comfort to the rebellious enemy without being bodily forced thereto.

156. Common justice and plain expediency require that the military commander protect the manifestly loyal citizens in revolted territories against the hardships of the war as much as the common misfortune of all war admits.

The commander will throw the burden of the war, as much as lies within his power, on the disloyal citizens, of the revolted portion or province, subjecting them to a stricter police than the non-combatant enemies have to suffer in regular war; and if he deems it appropriate, or if his government demands of him that every citizen shall, by an oath of allegiance, or by some other manifest act, declare his fidelity to the legitimate government, he may expel, transfer, imprison, or fine the revolted citizens who refuse to pledge themselves anew as citizens obedient to the law and loyal to the government.

Whether it is expedient to do so, and whether reliance can be placed upon such oaths, the commander or his government have the right to decide.

157. Armed or unarmed resistance by citizens of the United States against the lawful movements of their troops is levying war against the United States, and is therefore treason.

Appendix C

Proclamation Issued by Major General Arthur MacArthur on 20 December 1900*

PROCLAMATION

OFFICE OF U.S. MILITARY GOVERNOR
IN THE PHILIPPINE ISLANDS AND
HEADQUARTERS DIVISION OF THE PHILIPPINES,
Manila, P.I., December 10, 1900.

In the armed struggle against the sovereign power of the United States now in progress in these islands, frequent violations of important provisions of the laws of war have recently manifested themselves, rendering it imperative, while rejecting every consideration of belligerency of those opposing the Government in the sense in which the term belligerency is generally accepted and understood, to remind all concerned of the existence of these laws, that exemplary punishments attach to the infringment thereof, and that their strict observance is required not only by combatant forces, but as well by noncombatants, native or alien, residing within occupied places.

In pursuance of this purpose reference is made to the following provisions of the laws of war as most essential for consideration under present conditions:

I. A place, district, or country occupied in consequence of regular military operations by an organized combatant force stands, by reason of said occupation, under the martial law of the occupying army. The commanding general owes protection to all people residing within the places occupied, who perform with fidelity the duties imposed upon them, from which consideration results the obligation upon the part of the people and civil officials of the occupied territory of strict obedience to the commanding general of the occupying force.

The present necessity for allusion to the laws of war arises from the fact that many proclamations recently issued by insurgent commanders threaten punishment against all native inhabitants of occupied places who accept the reciprocal relations above described, and from the further fact

*Extract from *Affairs in the Philippine Islands. Hearings before the Committee on the Philippines of the United States Senate*. US Congress, Senate Document 331, Part 2, 57th Congress, 1st Session, 1902, pp 1944–1946.

that in prosecution of this policy the mandates of insurgent officers to kidnap and assassinate residents of occupied towns have been successfully executed. It can not, therefore, be too emphatically declared that all engaged in such transactions, from the authority making the proclamation to the parties of execution, are, collectively and individually, guilty of violation of the laws of war and must eventually answer for murder or such other crimes as may result from their unlawful actions.

Notice is accordingly given to insurgent leaders already committed to, or who may be contemplating such a system of war, that the practice thereof will necessarily terminate the possibility of those engaging therein returning to normal civic relations in the Philippines. That is to say, persons charged with violation of the laws of war above enumerated must sooner or later be tried for felonious crimes, with all the attending possibilities of conviction, or, as an only means of escape therefrom, must become fugitive criminals beyond the jurisdiction of the United States, which, in effect, means lifelong expatriation.

II. Persons residing within an occupied place who do things inimical to the interests of the occupying army are known as war rebels, or war traitors, according to the nature of their overt acts, and are punishable at the discretion of the tribunals of the occupying army. To comply with the demands of an expelled public enemy and make no report thereof creates the presumption that the act is voluntary and malicious. In such a case a plea of intimidation can rarely be accepted. The plain duty of people so threatened is to report the facts, which must, by reason of a common language, be of knowledge to a large part of the residential community, and thereby avert suspicion as to their own good faith and enable the commanding general to act efficiently in behalf of their protection. When, however, as is known to be the case in many places occupied by United States troops, secret committees are permitted to exist and to act in behalf of the so-called insurgent government by collecting supplies, recruiting men, and sending military information to the insurgent camps, it is not only difficult to afford adequate protection, but the well-disposed people who, from a sense of timidity or misplaced sympathy for neighbors, persist in screening these committees, in effect offer themselves as easy victims to be plundered and murdered, and also expose themselves to the danger of being classified and tried as war traitors against the United States.

The principal object of this proclamation is to instruct all classes throughout the archipelago as to the requirement of the laws of war in respect to the particulars herein referred to, and to advise all concerned of the purpose to exact in the future precise compliance therewith. The practice of sending supplies to insurgent troops from places occupied by the United States, as is now the case, must cease. If contumacious or faint-hearted persons continue to engage in this traffic, they must be prepared to answer for their actions under the penalties declared in this article.

III. The remarks embodied in the foregoing Article II apply with special force to the city of Manila, which is well known as a rendezvous from which an extensive correspondence is distributed to all parts of the archipelago by sympathizers with and by emissaries of the insurrection. All persons in Manila or elsewhere are again reminded that the entire archipelago, for the time being, is necessarily under the rigid restraints of martial law, and that any contributions of advice, information, or supplies, and all correspondence, the effect of which is to give aid, support, encouragement, or comfort to the armed opposition in the field are flagrant violations of American interests, and persons so engaged are warned to conform to the laws which apply to occupied places as herein set forth.

The newspapers and other periodicals of Manila, being of issue in an occupied place, are especially admonished that any article published in the midst of such martial environment which by any construction can be classed as seditious must be regarded as intended to injure the army of occupation, and as subjecting all connected with the publication to such punitive action as may be determined by the undersigned.

IV. Men who participate in hostilities without being part of a regularly organized force, and without sharing continuously in its operations, but who do so with intermittent returns to their homes and avocations, divest themselves of the character of soldiers, and if captured are not entitled to the privileges of prisoners of war.

It is well known that many of the occupied towns support and encourage men who habitually assume the semblance of peaceful pursuits, but who have arms hidden outside of the towns and periodically slip out to take part in guerrilla war.

The fact that such men have not heretofore been held responsible for their actions is simply an evidence of the solicitude of the United States to avoid all appearance of harshness in pacifying the islands, and not of any defect in the law itself. The people of the archipelago are now instructed as to the precise nature of the law applicable in such cases, and are warned to mistrust leaders who not only require soldiers to expose themselves to the ordinary vicissitudes of campaign, but insist upon duties that necessarily expose all who engage therein to the possibility of trial for a capital offense.

War in its earliest form was an act of violence which, from the very nature of primitive humanity and the forces employed, knew no bounds.

Mankind, from the beginning of civilization, however, has tried to mitigate, and to escape, as far as possible, from the consequences of this barbarous conception of warlike action; and to that end conventions have been held from time to time for international discussion of the customs and usages of war, in the hope that some means might be devised to regulate by rule the beneficent instincts of humanity. As a consequence of such conferences, a code has slowly evolved which, although uncertain in many particulars, contains certain fundamental principles which have been accepted and are now insisted upon by the public opinion of the world. The articles discussed in this paper have been adopted by all civilized nations. Their careful perusal by the people, it is hoped, will induce all who are eager for the tranquillization of the archipelago to combine for mutual protection and united action in behalf of their own interests and the welfare of the country.

ARTHUR MACARTHUR,
Major-General, U.S.V.,
U.S. Military Governor in the Philippines.

Appendix D

Extract of Message from President Theodore Roosevelt to the US Army, 4 July 1902*

War Department, *Washington, July 4, 1902.*

To the Army of the United States:

The President upon this anniversary of national independence wishes to express to the officers and enlisted men of the United States Army his deep appreciation of the service they have rendered to the country in the great and difficult undertakings which they have brought to a successful conclusion during the past year.

*   *   *   *   *   *   *

The President thanks the officers and enlisted men of the Army in the Philippines, both regulars and volunteers, for the courage and fortitude, the indomitable spirit and loyal devotion with which they have put down and ended the great insurrection which has raged throughout the archipelago against the lawful sovereignty and just authority of the United States. The task was peculiarly difficult and trying. They were required at first to overcome organized resistance of superior numbers, well equipped with modern arms of precision, intrenched in an unknown country of mountain defiles, jungles, and swamps, apparently capable of interminable defense. When this resistance had been overcome they were required to crush out a general system of guerrilla warfare conducted among a people speaking unknown tongues, from whom it was almost impossible to obtain the information necessary for successful pursuit or to guard against surprise and ambush.

The enemies by whom they were surrounded were regardless of all obligations of good faith and of all the limitations which humanity has imposed upon civilized warfare. Bound themselves by the laws of war, our soldiers were called upon to meet every device of unscrupulous treachery

---

*Headquarters of the Army, General Orders No. 66, 4 July 1902, in US Army, Adjutant General's Office, *Correspondence Relating to the War with Spain and Conditions Growing out of the Same Including the Insurrection in the Philippine Islands and the China Relief Expedition, Between the Adjutant-General of the Army and Military Commanders in the United States, Cuba, Porto Rico, China, and the Philippine Islands from April 15, 1898 to July 30, 1902* (Washington, DC: Government Printing Office, 1902), vol. II, 1352–1353.

and to contemplate without reprisal the infliction of barbarous cruelties upon their comrades and friendly natives. They were instructed, while punishing armed resistance, to conciliate the friendship of the peaceful, yet had to do with a population among whom it was impossible to distinguish friend from foe, and who in countless instances used a false appearance of friendship for ambush and assassination. They were obliged to deal with problems of communication and transportation in a country without roads and frequently made impassable by torrential rains. They were weakened by tropical heat and tropical disease. Widely scattered over a great archipelago, extending a thousand miles from north to south, the gravest responsibilities, involving the life or death of their commands, frequently devolved upon young and inexperienced officers beyond the reach of specific orders or advice.

Under all these adverse circumstances the Army of the Philippines has accomplished its task rapidly and completely. In more than two thousand combats, great and small, within three years, it has exhibited unvarying courage and resolution. Utilizing the lessons of the Indian wars, it has relentlessly followed the guerrilla bands to their fastnesses in mountain and jungle and crushed them. It has put an end to the vast system of intimidation and secret assassination by which the peaceful natives were prevented from taking a genuine part in government under American authority. It has captured or forced to surrender substantially all the leaders of the insurrection. It has submitted to no discouragement and halted at no obstacle. Its officers have shown high qualities of command, and its men have shown devotion and discipline. Its splendid virile energy has been accompanied by self-control, patience, and magnanimity. With surprisingly few individual exceptions its course has been characterized by humanity and kindness to the prisoner and the noncombatant. With admirable good temper, sympathy, and loyalty to American ideals its commanding generals have joined with civilian agents of the Government in healing the wounds of war and assuring to the people of the Philippines the blessings of peace and prosperity. Individual liberty, protection of personal rights, civil order, public instruction, and religious freedom have followed its footsteps. It has added honor to the flag which it defended, and has justified increased confidence in the future of the American people, whose soldiers do not shrink from labor or death, yet love liberty and peace.

The President feels that he expresses the sentiments of all the loyal people of the United States in doing honor to the whole Army which has joined in the performance and shares in the credit of these honorable services.

This general order will be read aloud at parade in every military post on the 4th day of July, 1902, or on the first day after it shall have been received.

Elihu Root, *Secretary of War.*

By command of Lieutenant-General Miles:

H.C. Corbin,
Adjutant-General, Major-General, U.S. Army.

About the Author

Robert D. Ramsey III retired from the US Army in 1993 after 24 years of service as an Infantry officer that included tours in Vietnam, Korea, and the Sinai. He earned an M.A. in history from Rice University. Mr. Ramsey taught military history for 3 years at the United States Military Academy and 6 years at the US Army Command and General Staff College. Mr. Ramsey is the author of Global War on Terrorism Occasional Paper 18, *Advising Indigenous Forces: American Advisors in Korea, Vietnam, and El Salvador;* and Occasional Paper 19, *Advice for Advisors: Suggestions and Observations from Lawrence to the Present.*

167